# Practice *Planners*

### Arthur E. Jongsma, Jr., Series Editor

## *Helping therapists help their clients...*

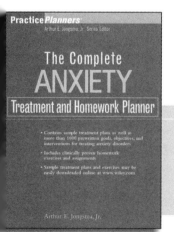

**Treatment Planners** cover all the necessary elements for developing formal treatment plans, including detailed problem definitions, long-term goals, short-term objectives, therapeutic interventions, and DSM-IV™ diagnoses.

❏ The Complete Adult Psychotherapy Treatment Planner, Fourth Edition........978-0-471-76346-8 / $55.00
❏ The Child Psychotherapy Treatment Planner, Fourth Edition .......................978-0-471-78535-4 / $55.00
❏ The Adolescent Psychotherapy Treatment Planner, Fourth Edition .............978-0-471-78539-2 / $55.00
❏ The Addiction Treatment Planner, Fourth Edition.......................................978-0-470-40551-2 / $55.00
❏ The Couples Psychotherapy Treatment Planner, Second Edition...................978-0-470-40695-3 / $55.00
❏ The Group Therapy Treatment Planner, Second Edition.................................978-0-471-66791-9 / $55.00
❏ The Family Therapy Treatment Planner, Second Edition................................978-0-470-44193-0 / $55.00
❏ The Older Adult Psychotherapy Treatment Planner .....................................978-0-471-29574-7 / $55.00
❏ The Employee Assistance (EAP) Treatment Planner .....................................978-0-471-24709-8 / $55.00
❏ The Gay and Lesbian Psychotherapy Treatment Planner ..............................978-0-471-35080-4 / $55.00
❏ The Crisis Counseling and Traumatic Events Treatment Planner ...............978-0-471-39587-4 / $55.00
❏ The Social Work and Human Services Treatment Planner ..........................978-0-471-37741-2 / $55.00
❏ The Continuum of Care Treatment Planner.................................................978-0-471-19568-9 / $55.00
❏ The Behavioral Medicine Treatment Planner ..............................................978-0-471-31923-8 / $55.00
❏ The Mental Retardation and Developmental Disability Treatment Planner ...978-0-471-38253-9 / $55.00
❏ The Special Education Treatment Planner....................................................978-0-471-38872-2 / $55.00
❏ The Severe and Persistent Mental Illness Treatment Planner, Second Edition....978-0-470-18013-6 / $55.00
❏ The Personality Disorders Treatment Planner .............................................978-0-471-39403-7 / $55.00
❏ The Rehabilitation Psychology Treatment Planner ......................................978-0-471-35178-8 / $55.00
❏ The Pastoral Counseling Treatment Planner...............................................978-0-471-25416-4 / $55.00
❏ The Juvenile Justice and Residential Care Treatment Planner ...................978-0-471-43320-0 / $55.00
❏ The School Counseling and School Social Work Treatment Planner ..........978-0-471-08496-9 / $55.00
❏ The Psychopharmacology Treatment Planner ..............................................978-0-471-43322-4 / $55.00
❏ The Probation and Parole Treatment Planner..............................................978-0-471-20244-8 / $55.00
❏ The Suicide and Homicide Risk Assessment & Prevention Treatment Planner ..978-0-471-46631-4 / $55.00
❏ The Speech-Language Pathology Treatment Planner....................................978-0-471-27504-6 / $55.00
❏ The College Student Counseling Treatment Planner ...................................978-0-471-46708-3 / $55.00
❏ The Parenting Skills Treatment Planner .....................................................978-0-471-48183-6 / $55.00
❏ The Early Childhood Education Intervention Treatment Planner ...............978-0-471-65962-4 / $55.00
❏ The Co-Occurring Disorders Treatment Planner.........................................978-0-471-73081-1 / $55.00
❏ The Sexual Abuse Victim and Sexual Offender Treatment Planner ............978-0-471-21979-8 / $55.00
❏ The Complete Women's Psychotherapy Treatment Planner ......................978-0-470-03983-0 / $55.00
❏ The Veterans and Active Duty Military Psychotherapy Treatment Planner ...978-0-470-44098-8 / $55.00

The **Complete Treatment and Homework Planners** series of books combines our bestselling *Treatment Planners* and *Homework Planners* into one easy-to-use, all-in-one resource for mental health professionals treating clients suffering from the most commonly diagnosed disorders.

❏ The Complete Depression Treatment and Homework Planner ...................978-0-471-64515-3 / $48.95
❏ The Complete Anxiety Treatment and Homework Planner .........................978-0-471-64548-1 / $48.95

## ver 500,000 Practice *Planners* sold ...

WILEY

# Family Therapy
# Homework Planner

# Practice*Planners*® Series

## Treatment Planners

*The Complete Adult Psychotherapy Treatment Planner, Fourth Edition*
*The Child Psychotherapy Treatment Planner, Fourth Edition*
*The Adolescent Psychotherapy Treatment Planner, Fourth Edition*
*The Addiction Treatment Planner, Fourth Edition*
*The Continuum of Care Treatment Planner*
*The Couples Psychotherapy Treatment Planner, Second Edition*
*The Employee Assistance Treatment Planner*
*The Pastoral Counseling Treatment Planner*
*The Older Adult Psychotherapy Treatment Planner*
*The Behavioral Medicine Treatment Planner*
*The Group Therapy Treatment Planner*
*The Gay and Lesbian Psychotherapy Treatment Planner*
*The Family Therapy Treatment Planner, Second Edition*
*The Severe and Persistent Mental Illness Treatment Planner, Second Edition*
*The Mental Retardation and Developmental Disability Treatment Planner*
*The Social Work and Human Services Treatment Planner*
*The Crisis Counseling and Traumatic Events Treatment Planner*
*The Personality Disorders Treatment Planner*
*The Rehabilitation Psychology Treatment Planner*
*The Special Education Treatment Planner*
*The Juvenile Justice and Residential Care Treatment Planner*
*The School Counseling and School Social Work Treatment Planner*
*The Sexual Abuse Victim and Sexual Offender Treatment Planner*
*The Probation and Parole Treatment Planner*
*The Psychopharmacology Treatment Planner*
*The Speech-Language Pathology Treatment Planner*
*The Suicide and Homicide Treatment Planner*
*The College Student Counseling Treatment Planner*
*The Parenting Skills Treatment Planner*
*The Early Childhood Intervention Treatment Planner*
*The Co-Occurring Disorders Treatment Planner*
*The Complete Women's Psychotherapy Treatment Planner*
*The Veterans and Active Duty Military Psychotherapy Treatment Planner*

## Progress Notes Planners

*The Child Psychotherapy Progress Notes Planner, Third Edition*
*The Adolescent Psychotherapy Progress Notes Planner, Third Edition*
*The Adult Psychotherapy Progress Notes Planner, Third Edition*
*The Addiction Progress Notes Planner, Third Edition*
*The Severe and Persistent Mental Illness Progress Notes Planner, Second Edition*
*The Couples Psychotherapy Progress Notes Planner*
*The Family Therapy Progress Notes Planner, Second Edition*
*The Veterans and Active Duty Military Psychotherapy Progress Notes Planner*

## Homework Planners

*Couples Therapy Homework Planner, Second Edition*
*Family Therapy Homework Planner, Second Edition*
*Grief Counseling Homework Planner*
*Group Therapy Homework Planner*
*Divorce Counseling Homework Planner*
*School Counseling and School Social Work Homework Planner*
*Child Therapy Activity and Homework Planner*
*Addiction Treatment Homework Planner, Fourth Edition*
*Adolescent Psychotherapy Homework Planner II*
*Adolescent Psychotherapy Homework Planner, Second Edition*
*Adult Psychotherapy Homework Planner, Second Edition*
*Child Psychotherapy Homework Planner, Second Edition*
*Parenting Skills Homework Planner*

## Client Education Handout Planners

*Adult Client Education Handout Planner*
*Child and Adolescent Client Education Handout Planner*
*Couples and Family Client Education Handout Planner*

## Complete Planners

*The Complete Depression Treatment and Homework Planner*
*The Complete Anxiety Treatment and Homework Planner*

Arthur E. Jongsma Jr., Series Editor

# Family Therapy Homework Planner

## Second Edition

*Louis J. Bevilacqua*

*and*

*Frank M. Dattilio*

WILEY

John Wiley & Sons, Inc.

This book is printed on acid-free paper. ∞

Published by John Wiley & Sons, Inc., Hoboken, New Jersey.

Published simultaneously in Canada.

This publication is designed to provide accurate and authoritative information in regard to the subject matter covered. It is sold with the understanding that the publisher is not engaged in rendering professional services. If legal, accounting, medical, psychological or any other expert assistance is required, the services of a competent professional person should be sought.

Designations used by companies to distinguish their products are often claimed as trademarks. In all instances where John Wiley & Sons, Inc. is aware of a claim, the product names appear in initial capital or all capital letters. Readers, however, should contact the appropriate companies for more complete information regarding trademarks and registration.

For general information on our other products and services please contact our Customer Care Department within the U.S. at (800) 762-2974, outside the United States at (317) 572-3993 or fax (317) 572-4002.

Wiley also publishes its books in a variety of electronic formats. Some content that appears in print may not be available in electronic books. For more information about Wiley products, visit our web site at www.wiley.com.

*Library of Congress Cataloging-in-Publication Data:*
Bevilacqua, Louis.
  Family therapy homework planner / by Louis J. Bevilacqua and Frank M. Dattilio. — 2nd ed.
    p. cm. — (PracticePlanners series)
  Includes bibliographical references.
  ISBN 978-0-470-50439-0 (paper/cd-rom : alk. paper); ISBN 978-0-470-63833-0 (ebk);
  ISBN 978-0-470-63834-7 (ebk); 978-0-470-63836-1 (ebk)
    1. Family psychotherapy—Problems, exercises, etc. 2. Brief psychotherapy—Problems, exercises, etc.
  3. Mental illness—Treatment. I. Dattilio, Frank M. II. Title.

RC488.5.B493 2010

616.89'156—dc22
                                                                        2010000765

Printed in the United States of America.

10 9 8 7 6 5 4 3 2

*To my wife and best friend Debbie Bevilacqua and our
three beautiful daughters, Rachael, Amanda, and Lindsey.
Thanks for all your love and support.*

*Louis J. Bevilacqua*


*To my wife, children, and grandchildren.
You are truly the light of my life.*

*Frank M. Dattilio*

# CONTENTS

# PRACTICE*PLANNERS*® SERIES PREFACE

Accountability is an important dimension of the practice of psychotherapy. Treatment programs, public agencies, clinics, and practitioners must justify and document their treatment plans to outside review entities in order to be reimbursed for services. The books and software in the Practice*Planners*® series are designed to help practitioners fulfill these documentation requirements efficiently and professionally.

The Practice*Planners*® series includes a wide array of treatment planning books, including not only the original *Complete Adult Psychotherapy Treatment Planner, Child Psychotherapy Treatment Planner,* and *Adolescent Psychotherapy Treatment Planner,* all now in their fourth editions, but also *Treatment Planners* targeted to specialty areas of practice, including:

- Addictions
- Co-occurring disorders
- Behavioral medicine
- College students
- Couples therapy
- Crisis counseling
- Early childhood education
- Employee assistance
- Family therapy
- Gays and lesbians
- Group therapy
- Juvenile justice and residential care
- Mental retardation and developmental disability
- Neuropsychology
- Older adults
- Parenting skills
- Pastoral counseling
- Personality disorders
- Probation and parole
- Psychopharmacology
- Rehabilitation psychology
- School counseling
- Severe and persistent mental illness
- Sexual abuse victims and offenders
- Social work and human services

- Special education
- Speech-language pathology
- Suicide and homicide risk assessment
- Women's issues

In addition, there are three branches of companion books which can be used in conjunction with the *Treatment Planners*, or on their own:

- ***Progress Notes Planners*** provide a menu of progress statements that elaborate on the client's symptom presentation and the provider's therapeutic intervention. Each *Progress Notes Planner* statement is directly integrated with the behavioral definitions and therapeutic interventions from its companion *Treatment Planner*.

- ***Homework Planners*** include homework assignments designed around each presenting problem (such as anxiety, depression, chemical dependence, anger management, eating disorders, or panic disorder) that is the focus of a chapter in its corresponding *Treatment Planner*.

- ***Client Education Handout Planners*** provide brochures and handouts to help educate and inform clients on presenting problems and mental health issues, as well as life skills techniques. The handouts are included on CD-ROMs for easy printing from your computer and are ideal for use in waiting rooms, at presentations, as newsletters, or as information for clients struggling with mental illness issues. The topics covered by these handouts correspond to the presenting problems in the *Treatment Planners*.

The series also includes:

- **Thera*Scribe*®**, the #1- selling treatment planning and clinical record-keeping software system for mental health professionals. Thera*Scribe*® allows the user to import the data from any of the *Treatment Planner*, *Progress Notes Planner*, or *Homework Planner* books into the software's expandable database to simply point and click to create a detailed, organized, individualized, and customized treatment plan along with optional integrated progress notes and homework assignments.

Adjunctive books, such as *The Psychotherapy Documentation Primer* and *The Clinical Documentation Sourcebook*, contain forms and resources to aid the clinician in mental health practice management.

The goal of our series is to provide practitioners with the resources they need in order to provide high quality care in the era of accountability. To put it simply: We seek to help you spend more time on patients, and less time on paperwork.

ARTHUR E. JONGSMA, JR.
*Grand Rapids, Michigan*

# ACKNOWLEDGMENTS

The challenging task of assembling a manuscript such as this one is not possible without the contributions of many individuals working on the sidelines.

First and foremost, we would like to thank the many families who have provided us with our vast experiences during our years of clinical work. This has allowed us to generate a number of effective assignments that are contained in the text. It is only after much trial and error that we are able to sort out what works and what does not, and convey it in a manner that can be applied clinically.

In addition, we would like to give hearty thanks to our expert typist, Carol Jaskolka, who has devoted a great deal of time and energy to preparing the manuscript and assembling the various chapters. For this, we are greatly indebted to her. Many thanks also go to Marquita Flemming, Senior Editor, and Peggy Alexander, Vice President and Publisher, at John Wiley & Sons, Inc. We are grateful to them for their trust and patience with us to provide a first-rate manuscript.

Last, our greatest thanks are extended to our own families, who have been undyingly supportive to us as we practice what we preach, despite the time and attention they were deprived of during the completion of this manuscript.

Louis J. Bevilacqua
Frank M. Dattilio

# INTRODUCTION

Family therapists are assigning homework to their clients on a more regular basis due to the evidence-based movement that has now become a gold standard in the field. Not only have short-term psychotherapy models endorsed the use of homework, but the benefits are continuing to be recognized by many of the more traditional family therapists as well.

## A RATIONALE FOR HOMEWORK ASSIGNMENTS

Since the first edition of the *Family Therapy Homework Planner,* additional research studies have been published on the efficacy of homework assignments in treatment.

Homework assignments are an efficacious clinical tool with strong theoretical and practical support. Between-session tasks have been well documented in the professional literature and assist with the reinforcement, maintenance, and generalization of skills learned during the course and content of therapy (Kellogg & Young, 2008; Zinbarg & Griffith, 2008). More recently, homework assignments have particularly begun to show strong evidence of effectiveness in work with couples and families (Dattilio & Dickson, 2007; Epstein & Baucom, 2007; L'Abate & Cusinato, 2007; Lindille & Hertlein, 2007). Empirical research has demonstrated that many couples and family therapists of various modalities do indeed use a variety of homework assignments with both couples and families and view the utility of such to be significant (Dattilio, Kazantzis, Shinkfield, & Carr, 2010; Dattilio, Carr, & Kazantzis, in press).

Assigning homework to couples and families is beneficial for a number of reasons. For one, research documents that it aids in maximizing the effectiveness of briefer treatments employed and allows therapists to assign homework as an extension of the treatment process, as well as providing continuity. It also allows families to work on issues that are the focus of therapy in between sessions, which serves to galvanize the treatment process (Dattilio, 2010). This is particularly important in managed-care situations, which often require shorter and fewer treatment sessions. Homework can also be utilized as a tool to more fully engage family members during the course of treatment. This allows the family to assume more responsibility and move away from the notion that the therapist is the healer. Homework assignments nicely underscore collaboration between therapists and clients.

Homework is also essential in that assignments can be crafted in a manner that provides an opportunity for families to implement and evaluate insights or coping behaviors that have been processed during the course of therapy. Homework assignments also increase the expectation for family members to follow through with making change rather than simply discussing it as a goal. Homework assignments often create a sense of having family members take active steps towards the facilitation of change. This further facilitates the stage for trial experiences, which can be discussed in the subsequent sessions, allowing for modifications to be made.

It is not unusual for treatment processes to become vague and somewhat abstract, which dilutes the overall impact of treatment. By fortifying therapy sessions with focus and structure, homework assignments allow for the re-energizing of the treatment process. At times, when the therapist may encounter barriers or resistance, homework may also serve to increase a family member's motivation to change or work through obstacles and narrow down the focus on the impediments in growth.

Two other additional benefits include the increased involvement of family members and significant others in the client's treatment by way of assignments that call for the participation of others and the promotion of more efficient treatment by encouraging the family members to actively develop insights, positive self-talk, and coping behaviors between therapy sessions. Families are often thrilled to be given something active to do, which facilitates the change process and reinforces their sense of control and mastery over a particular problem. As a result of these advantages, the assignment of therapeutic homework has become increasingly utilized and has also been found to be effective in outcome studies.

## HOW TO USE THIS HOMEWORK PLANNER

Creating homework assignments and developing the printed forms for recording responses can be a time-consuming process. The *Family Therapy Homework Planner,* which follows the lead of psychotherapeutic interventions suggested in the *Family Therapy Treatment Planner* (Dattilio & Jongsma, 2010), was written to provide a menu of homework assignments that can easily be photocopied. In addition to the printed format, the assignments in this *Planner* are provided on a disk to allow the therapist to open them in a word processor and subsequently print them out or quickly custom-tailor them to suit each client's individual needs and the therapist's unique style.

The assignments are grouped under presenting problems that are typical of those found in familial situations. These presenting problems are cross-referenced to most of the presenting problems found in the *Family Therapy Treatment Planner.* Although these assignments were originally created with a specific presenting problem in mind, don't feel locked in by specific behavioral problems. Included with each exercise is a cross-referenced list of suggested presenting problems for which the assignment may be appropriate and useful. This cross-referenced list can assist you in applying the assignments to other situations that may be relevant to your client's particular presenting problem.

## ABOUT THE ASSIGNMENTS

Some of the assignments are designed for the parents of families who are in treatment; others may be for individual family members, such as the child; still others are designed for the parents and adolescent to complete together. Therapists will have to introduce the therapy assignment with varying degrees of detail and client preparation. Recommendations regarding this preparation are made on the title page of each assignment under the heading "Suggestions for Processing This Exercise with Client."

When using this sourcebook, clinical judgment must be used to assess the appropriate developmental level necessary for a specific assignment, as well as whether the homework focuses on relevant issues for the client. The title page of each assignment contains a section on "Goals of the Exercise," which should guide you in your selection of relevant homework for your clients. Remember, all assignments can be modified as necessary to fit the need of each family.

## CARRYING OUT THE ASSIGNMENT

It is recommended that you first peruse the entire book of homework assignments to familiarize yourself with the broad nature of the types and focuses of the homework. When the time arrives, select a specific assignment under a presenting problem and review the list of homework objectives. Assigning therapy homework is just a beginning step in the treatment process. Carrying out the assignment requires an exploration, on your end as well as the client's, to find the conclusions at which the client has arrived. What are the results? Was this assignment useful to the client? Can it be redesigned or altered for better results? Feel free to examine and search for new and creative ways to actively engage your client in participating in this homework process.

LOUIS J. BEVILACQUA
FRANK M. DATTILIO

# WHEN CAN WE BE TOGETHER?

## GOALS OF THE EXERCISE

1. To find an acceptable balance between the competing demands of external activities and family responsibilities.
2. Reduce family tension/stress related to lack of family time.

## ADDITIONAL HOMEWORK THAT MAY BE APPLICABLE TO EXTERNAL ACTIVITIES AFFECTING FAMILY ROLE

- Acting as If                                          Page 52
- Everything Is Always Negative in Our House           Page 92
- Why Can't You Understand My Side for Once?           Pages 164, 166

## ADDITIONAL PROBLEMS IN WHICH THIS EXERCISE MAY BE USEFUL

- Poor Communication
- Disengagement
- Jealousy
- Anger

## SUGGESTIONS FOR PROCESSING THIS EXERCISE WITH FAMILY MEMBERS

Many families have difficulty finding time for each other. Children are often involved in numerous activities, and very often both parents are working. As a result, family time is competing with a multitude of other activities and demands. The following activity is designed to help families create time for the family as a whole.

# WHEN CAN WE BE TOGETHER?

The following exercise is designed to help family members create time for the family as a whole. Each of you will need some paper and a pen or pencil. During a family meeting, respond to the following statements.

1.  Each family member is to express his/her priorities regarding how time is spent (e.g., family time, work, individual time, friends, etc.).
2.  Each family member should rank-order these priorities according to most important to least important.
3.  Approximately how much time is currently being spent on each priority?
4.  Each family member is to express his/her feelings regarding the lack of time spent together as a family or with a particular family member.
5.  Have each family member describe how much time he/she would like to spend as a family or with that particular family member.
6.  As a family, brainstorm a list of possible family activities that might be considered (e.g., monthly family night out or night in, weekly family meetings to touch base with others and share how his/her week has been, monthly lunch date with Dad, monthly shopping trip with Mom).
7.  As a family, use a calendar to select some dates as to when and what you will do together.

# HOW MUCH DOES IT COST?

## GOALS OF THE EXERCISE

1. To help break through the level of denial to addiction.
2. To increase motivation to achieve and/or maintain sobriety.

## ADDITIONAL HOMEWORK THAT MAY BE APPLICABLE TO ALCOHOL ABUSE

- It's Us Against the Anxiety          Page 38
- Creating a Positive Outlook          Page 227
- What Am I Thinking?                   Page 128

## ADDITIONAL PROBLEMS FOR WHICH THIS EXERCISE MAY BE USEFUL

- Activity/Family Imbalance
- Anger Management
- Blaming
- Compulsive Behaviors
- Jealousy/Insecurity

## SUGGESTIONS FOR PROCESSING THIS EXERCISE WITH CLIENT

Individuals who struggle with addictive-like behaviors often justify to themselves why the behavior is okay. This exercise can be used to help individuals challenge such rationalizations and increase their awareness of reality. It can also be used with individuals who feel stuck or doubt the purpose of changing a behavior.

# HOW MUCH DOES IT COST?

Have you ever wondered how much your behavior costs you? In addition to financial cost, addictive behavior can also cost you in many other ways. To find out how, complete the following exercise.

In any addictive process, individuals will spend time thinking about the behavior, conjuring rationalizations to try to make the behavior occur, engage in the behavior, experience the effects of the behavior, and experience the after effects. As in any situation, what one does will have an effect on those around him or her. When someone is in a bad mood, and they respond to you in a grouchy tone of voice or with short one-word answers, this will affect you. Perhaps it will make you want to respond in a similar manner. Perhaps it will make you want to leave and not be around that person. In a similar fashion, addictive behaviors affect others.

Think about the last time you engaged in your addictive behavior. Describe what the behavior was/is. _____

_____

_____

_____

a. Approximately how much time did you spend thinking about it before you actually did it? _____

b. What else could you have been doing?

_____

_____

_____

c. How much time did you spend doing the behavior? _____

d. What was your support system doing while you were engaging in your addictive behavior? (Ask them if you don't know.)

_____

_____

_____

e.  How much money did it cost you? _____

f.  What else could you have purchased with that amount of money?

_____

_____

_____

g.  What were the PHYSICAL effects of your addictive behavior?

_____

_____

_____

_____

_____

h.  How long did the PHYSICAL effects last? _____

i.  What else could you have done with that time?

_____

_____

_____

j.  How has your addictive behavior affected you at work?
Relationships: _____

_____

_____

Productivity: _____

_____

_____

Health: _____

_____

_____

Attendance: _____

_____

_____

Other: _____

_____

_____

k.  How has your addictive behavior HURT your relationships with family members?

_____

_____

_____

_____

_____

_____

l.  How has your addictive behavior HURT your relationship with friends?

_____

_____

_____

_____

_____

_____

m.  How has your addictive behavior hurt your body?

_____

_____

_____

_____

_____

_____

n.  How has your addictive behavior affected your decision making/choices?

_____

_____

_____

_____

_____

_____

# STAYING CLEAN

## GOALS OF THE EXERCISE

1. Identify triggers to relapse.
2. Provide greater understanding and insight for nonaddicted family members.

## ADDITIONAL HOMEWORK THAT MAY BE APPLICABLE TO STAYING CLEAN

- What Am I Thinking?                Page 128
- Creating a Positive Outlook        Page 227

## ADDITIONAL PROBLEMS FOR WHICH THIS EXERCISE MAY BE USEFUL

- Anxiety
- Social Problems*
- Stealing Behaviors*

## SUGGESTIONS FOR PROCESSING THIS EXERCISE WITH CLIENT

When a member of the family has an addiction, it affects the entire family in a variety of ways. There are many ways in which family members can help the individual who is in recovery. One of the steps to recovery is for the addicted individual to identify specific triggers to substance use. After identifying these triggers, they should be shared with the family. This provides greater insight and understanding for the nonaddicted members of the family. It also helps the recovering individual begin to take control of his/her life by becoming aware of and acknowledging those factors that lead his or her behaviors to be out of control.

In the exercise that follows, the recovering member is asked to answer a number of questions. Once completed, his/her answers should be shared with the therapist during an individual session and then with other family members.

---

*These problems are not specifically discussed in detail in this volume.

# STAYING CLEAN

## FOR THE RECOVERING FAMILY MEMBER

One of the best ways for you to prevent relapse is to become aware of the triggers to your need to use. Once you can identify these triggers, you may begin to feel more control over your life. Knowing what the triggers are can aid you in developing a stronger preventative plan to relapse. In this exercise, answer the following questions. Once completed, this exercise should be shared during an individual session with the therapist and then with other family members.

Describe the last five situations in which you used substance by answering the following questions:

1. Who were you with?

   _____
   _____
   _____

2. Where were you?

   _____
   _____
   _____

3. What time of the day was it?

   _____
   _____
   _____

4. How were you feeling before you chose to get high?

   _____
   _____
   _____

5.  What were you thinking about before you got high?

    _____

    _____

    _____

6.  What were your thoughts/feelings about that person or those people you were with?

    _____

    _____

    _____

7.  What did the substance do for you?

    _____

    _____

    _____

8.  What were you able to avoid by using the substance (e.g., feelings, hassles, people, situations, responsibilities)?

    _____

    _____

    _____

9.  How much do you believe others are responsible for your addictive habits?

    _____

    _____

    _____

# WHAT ELSE CAN I DO?

## GOALS OF THE EXERCISE

1. Identify alternative strategies to dealing with triggers to relapse.
2. Create reasons to remain clean.
3. List those thoughts and behaviors that you need to change.

## ADDITIONAL HOMEWORK THAT MAY BE APPLICABLE TO CLIENTS WITH AN ADDICTION

- What Am I Thinking?                Page 128
- Creating a Positive Outlook        Page 227

## ADDITIONAL PROBLEMS IN WHICH THIS EXERCISE MAY BE USEFUL

- Eating Disorders
- School Problems
- Stealing Behaviors[*]

## SUGGESTIONS FOR PROCESSING THIS EXERCISE WITH CLIENT

Once triggers are identified, new coping skills and strategies must be implemented to reduce the chances of relapse. Addiction is overwhelmingly powerful and can destroy individual lives and families. This cannot be emphasized enough. When an individual in recovery begins to have cravings or experience stress/triggers, the thoughts and desires to use quickly reappear. During these times individuals must be reminded of the benefits of staying clean and that other options are available for dealing with whatever problems they are encountering.

---

[*]This problem is not specifically discussed in detail in this volume.

# WHAT ELSE CAN I DO?

## FOR THE RECOVERING FAMILY MEMBER AND HIS/HER FAMILY

As a family project, select a stack of index cards. Each family member should write down one or more reasons s/he doesn't want the recovering member to relapse and how s/he feels about the recovering person when that individual is clean. The recovering member should do this as well. In the next family session, each person will take turns reading his or her card aloud.

Another way to help someone remain clean is by instituting "Caring Days."* Every so often, a family member does something caring for the recovering person (as well as for any other family member). The member who is in recovery can also participate by doing something caring for him or herself as well as for someone in the family in order to invoke an ongoing exchange.

One other family project can be to use another stack of index cards or select a family member to record on a legal pad a list of activities to do when experiencing cravings/urges to engage in an addictive/compulsive behavior.

---

*This was originally an exercise developed by Richard Stuart (1980) for use with couples. It is adapted here and elsewhere (Dattilio & Jongsma, 2000) to be used with families.

# KEEPING BUSY

## GOALS OF THE EXERCISE

1. Addicted or compulsive behavior is reduced or eliminated.
2. Family members feel that their concerns have been validated by the efforts of the addicted member to follow the activity schedule.

## ADDITIONAL HOMEWORK THAT MAY BE APPLICABLE TO CLIENTS WITH AN ADDICTION

- What Am I Thinking?            Page 128
- Creating a Positive Outlook    Page 227

## ADDITIONAL PROBLEMS IN WHICH THIS EXERCISE MAY BE USEFUL

- Depression
- Obsessive Type Behaviors
- Stealing Behaviors

## SUGGESTIONS FOR PROCESSING THIS EXERCISE WITH CLIENT

When a family member's behavior becomes so excessive or obsessive that it interferes with their daily or weekly activities or functioning, it can be an addiction. Various inventories can be used (such as the Daily Activity Sheet or Addictive Behaviors Scale) in order to identify a level of severity. Once this is accomplished and the addictive behavior is identified, family members need the opportunity to voice their perspectives on the negative effects that the addictive behavior has had on the family in general. This can be done in a family session. Usually, family members then want the identified behavior to be eliminated or at least reduced. One way to do this is by following a structured format to regulate behaviors.

# KEEPING BUSY

## FOR THE RECOVERING FAMILY MEMBER

One way for you to reduce or to hopefully eliminate unwanted behaviors is to create a daily activity schedule. Having a daily activity schedule or action plan allows you to schedule activities that you know are good for you.

Make a list of healthy activities. This can be done with the support of others by brainstorming together as many activities as you can generate. Once you have composed a list, select several activities and schedule them for the next week. After engaging in each activity, discuss what you liked and disliked about it. If it wasn't as good as you had hoped, describe what you could have done to improve it. Share your activity schedule and your responses to each activity with your support system.

Activities that I can choose to do:

| ACTIVITY SCHEDULE FOR THE WEEK | | | | | | | |
|---|---|---|---|---|---|---|---|
| Time | Sunday | Monday | Tuesday | Wednesday | Thursday | Friday | Saturday |
| 6AM | | | | | | | |
| 7AM | | | | | | | |
| 8AM | | | | | | | |
| 9AM | | | | | | | |
| 10AM | | | | | | | |
| 11AM | | | | | | | |
| Noon | | | | | | | |
| 1PM | | | | | | | |
| 2PM | | | | | | | |
| 3PM | | | | | | | |
| 4PM | | | | | | | |
| 5PM | | | | | | | |

| Time | Sunday | Monday | Tuesday | Wednesday | Thursday | Friday | Saturday |
|------|--------|--------|---------|-----------|----------|--------|----------|
| 6PM | | | | | | | |
| 7PM | | | | | | | |
| 8PM | | | | | | | |
| 9PM | | | | | | | |

| ACTIVITY RATING CHART | | |
|------|----------|---------------------------------------------|
| Date | Activity | What was good? How could it have been better? |
| | | |
| | | |
| | | |
| | | |
| | | |
| | | |
| | | |
| | | |
| | | |
| | | |
| | | |
| | | |
| | | |
| | | |
| | | |
| | | |

# THIS IS HOW I FEEL

## GOALS OF THE EXERCISE

1. The adopted child expresses feelings associated with being adopted.
2. Adopted child believes other family members understand how he or she is feeling.
3. All family members verbalize positive feelings toward one another.
4. Parents achieve positive feelings about their role as adoptive parents.

## ADDITIONAL HOMEWORK THAT MAY BE APPLICABLE TO ADOPTION

- A Picture Is Worth a Thousand Words (just pictures 1–3)    Page 215
- They're Calling Me a Half-Breed    Page 158
- Creating a Positive Outlook    Page 227

## ADDITIONAL PROBLEMS FOR WHICH THIS EXERCISE MAY BE USEFUL

- Blended Families
- Foster Care

## SUGGESTIONS FOR PROCESSING THIS EXERCISE WITH CLIENT

One of the most significant issues for a person who has been adopted is the need for acceptance and attachment or belonging. This is often the heart of the reason why an adoptive child/adolescent experiences struggles and needs to seek treatment.

For younger children, the exercise questions might be answered more easily and with greater depth via drawings or other expressive modalities. For children or adolescents who do not like to write, ask them to record their responses on an audiotape or via another form of expressive art (e.g., computer, phone).

# THIS IS HOW I FEEL

## FOR ADOPTIVE CHILD/ADOLESCENT

Being adopted can create a number of different thoughts and feelings. The exercise below will help you to identify and express such thoughts and feelings. If you would rather not write down your responses, try drawing them or recording them on an audio tape.

1.  Give three or four reasons why children are adopted.

    _____

    _____

    _____

    _____

2.  Explain the circumstances of how you were adopted. How did it happen?

    _____

    _____

    _____

    _____

    _____

3.  What type(s) of people adopt children?

    _____

    _____

    _____

    _____

    _____

4. What type of contact should an adopted child have with his/her biological family?

   _____

   _____

   _____

   _____

   _____

5. When you think about your biological family, what thoughts and feelings do you experience? Would you classify these as either positive or negative thoughts/emotions? _____

   _____

   _____

   _____

   _____

   _____

6. When you think about your adoptive family, what thoughts and feelings do you have? Would you classify these as either positive or negative thoughts/emotions?

   _____

   _____

   _____

   _____

   _____

# MY SAFE PLACE

## GOALS OF THE EXERCISE

1. To develop a sense of security and comfort no matter where you are or what time it is.
2. To be able to focus and reassure yourself that you are okay.
3. To be able to access that safe place whenever you feel frightened or insecure.

## ADDITIONAL HOMEWORK THAT MAY BE APPLICABLE TO ADOPTION

- Creating a Positive Outlook                                    Page 227
- They're Calling Me a Half-Breed                                Page 158
- A Picture Is Worth a Thousand Words (just pictures 1–3)        Page 215

## ADDITIONAL PROBLEMS FOR WHICH THIS EXERCISE MAY BE USEFUL

- Blended Families
- Child Sexual Abuse
- Depression
- Foster Care

## SUGGESTIONS FOR PROCESSING THIS EXERCISE WITH CLIENT

A safe place can be anywhere a person feels protected and able to truly relax without worrying. Through the use of imagery and visualization, a person can ideally access their safe place anytime, day or night, no matter where they are or whom they are with.

Before this task can be assigned, several sessions must be conducted in order to teach deep breathing and basic relaxation skills. After practicing and learning how to use diaphragmatic breathing,* explore with your client what type of place makes him/her feel good, comfortable, and calm. (Younger children may express places in which there are lots of activities and games. Redirect them to focus on places that are peaceful and quiet. Such places might be their bedroom or a tree house.) Facilitate the use of their imagination as much as possible.

Once a place is identified, have your client go there before their next appointment and spend approximately 10 to 15 minutes. Have them record as many details as possible about their safe place.

---

*With younger children, this can be taught by having them blow bubbles. The slower and longer the breath, the larger the bubbles one can make.

# MY SAFE PLACE

## FOR ADOPTIVE CHILD/ADOLESCENT

Feeling safe is a great feeling to have. Sometimes we are lucky enough to have a place where we can go and feel totally protected from anything and everything we don't like. It can be a real place like our room, our tree fort, the park, or on our bike. Or, it can be a place we can picture in our mind. A place in which we decide what it looks like, what it smells like, how big or small it is, what is in it, who, if anyone else, gets to visit. For the exercise below, try to think about what makes you feel safe. Where would it be? Try to picture it. Use the questions to describe your safe place.

1. My special safe place is:

   _____

   _____

   _____

   _____

   _____

2. Describe your safe place. (What does it look like? What does it smell like? How big is it? What is in it? What color is it?)

   _____

   _____

   _____

   _____

   _____

3. I feel safe there because:

   _____

   _____

   _____

   _____

   _____

# IS IT PASSIVE, AGGRESSIVE, OR ASSERTIVE?

## GOALS OF THE EXERCISE

1. Develop a clearer understanding of what it means to be assertive, passive, and aggressive.
2. Define these terms for yourself first and then compare what you have generated with traditional definitions (see Emmons & Alberti, 2007).
3. Be able to cite examples, that depict assertive, passive, and aggressive behaviors.

## ADDITIONAL HOMEWORK THAT MAY BE APPLICABLE TO ANGER MANAGEMENT

- My Safe Place                                             Page 19
- What Am I Thinking About When I Feel Depressed?           Page 115

## ADDITIONAL PROBLEMS IN WHICH THIS EXERCISE MAY BE USEFUL

- Dependency
- Anxiety

## SUGGESTIONS FOR PROCESSING THIS EXERCISE WITH CLIENT

Individuals who struggle with anger management tend to be either aggressive or passive. A goal of treatment is to help them achieve a middle ground between the two. In order to reach this goal it is important to decipher how each behavior is different. Individuals also need to increase their awareness of how they tend to respond. In a family session, process the differences of each behavior by defining and acting it out (e.g., role-play or model). Once each member has a clear understanding of the differences, suggest the following exercise, which will help them recognize these behaviors in their daily life.

# IS IT PASSIVE, AGGRESSIVE, OR ASSERTIVE?

In order for you to develop assertiveness, it is important to understand not only what it means to be assertive, but also what it means to be passive or aggressive and how frustration and anger is processed (see "Angry All the Time," from Dr. Weisenbergers' Anger Workbook). After you have discussed such differences in treatment, complete the following exercise.

Define each:

To be passive means to:

_____

_____

_____

An example of someone being passive is:

_____

_____

_____

To be aggressive means to:

_____

_____

_____

An example of someone being aggressive is:

_____

_____

_____

To be assertive means to:

_____

_____

_____

An example of someone being assertive is:

_____

_____

_____

Over the next week, each family member can use the following format to track his/her behavior. Record the date and describe the situation surrounding your behavior first and then describe how you responded or acted. Tell whether you were passive, aggressive, or assertive and why you think so. If you did not respond in an assertive manner, describe why and how you could next time.

Date _____

Situation:

_____

_____

_____

What I did in this situation:

_____

_____

_____

This was _____ because _____

_____

_____

_____

If this was not an assertive response, describe what prevented you from being assertive (e.g., if you were aggressive you may have been thinking, "That's not fair"; "s/he should have just listened to me." If you were being passive, you may have thought, "He or she would get mad at me" or "He or she would not like me" or "It wouldn't have made a difference").

_____

_____

_____

Describe how you could have responded in an assertive manner if you did not have those negative thoughts or fears.

_____

_____

_____

Date _____

Situation:

_____

_____

_____

What I did in this situation:

_____

_____

_____

This was _____ because _____

_____

_____

_____

I acted (aggressive/passive) because I was thinking _____

_____

_____

_____

Describe what thoughts you needed to have in order to have acted assertive.

_____

_____

_____

Date _____

Situation:

_____

_____

_____

What I did in this situation:

_____

_____

_____

This was _____ because _____

_____

_____

_____

I acted (aggressive/passive) because I was thinking _____

_____

_____

_____

Describe what thoughts you needed to have in order to have acted assertive.

_____

_____

_____


Date _____

Situation:

_____

_____

_____

What I did in this situation:

_____

_____

_____

This was _____ because _____

_____

_____

_____

I acted (aggressive/passive) because I was thinking _____

_____

_____

_____

Describe what thoughts you needed to have in order to have acted assertive.

_____

_____

_____

# WHY AM I SO ANGRY?

## GOALS OF THE EXERCISE

1. For family members to identify the sources of their anger.
2. For family members to identify the frequency of becoming angry and what they do.

## ADDITIONAL HOMEWORK THAT MAY BE APPLICABLE TO ANGER PROBLEMS

- My Safe Place                                                    Page 19
- What Am I Thinking When I Am Feeling Depressed?                  Page 115
- Creating a Positive Outlook                                      Page 227

## ADDITIONAL PROBLEMS FOR WHICH THIS EXERCISE MAY BE USEFUL

- Anxiety
- Depression

## SUGGESTIONS FOR PROCESSING THIS EXERCISE WITH CLIENT

Individuals who have difficulty with managing their anger are oftentimes unaware of just how often they become angry or why. The exercise on the following pages is designed to help such individuals increase their anger awareness. The more awareness they develop, the more it will allow them to have greater self-control.

# WHY AM I SO ANGRY?

## FOR CHILD/ADOLESCENT EXPERIENCING ANGER PROBLEMS

1.  For one week, use the chart provided to keep track of the times you become angry.

| Date | Time | Trigger | My Reaction | Thoughts or Feelings After |
|------|------|---------|-------------|----------------------------|
|      |      |         |             |                            |
|      |      |         |             |                            |
|      |      |         |             |                            |
|      |      |         |             |                            |
|      |      |         |             |                            |
|      |      |         |             |                            |
|      |      |         |             |                            |
|      |      |         |             |                            |

2.  Using the chart, identify the three top reasons for your becoming angry.

    a. _____

    _____

    _____

    b. _____

    _____

    _____

    c. _____

    _____

    _____

# WHAT HAPPENS WHEN I BECOME ANGRY?

## GOALS OF THE EXERCISE

1.  To identify the physiological, cognitive, emotional, and behavioral signs of anger.
2.  To begin to develop a sense of how others perceive an individual's anger.

## ADDITIONAL HOMEWORK THAT MAY BE APPLICABLE TO ANGER PROBLEMS

- My Safe Place                                              Page 19
- What Am I Thinking When I Am Feeling Depressed?            Page 115
- Creating a Positive Outlook                                Page 227

## ADDITIONAL PROBLEMS FOR WHICH THIS EXERCISE MAY BE USEFUL

- Anxiety

## SUGGESTIONS FOR PROCESSING THIS EXERCISE WITH CLIENT

When people become angry, it is important for them to become aware of their bodily reactions, thought patterns, emotions, and actual behaviors. By increasing his/her awareness of these undesirable factors, a person can begin to take control and reduce them.

# WHAT HAPPENS WHEN I BECOME ANGRY?

## FOR CHILD/ADOLESCENT EXPERIENCING ANGER PROBLEMS

For you to change what happens when you become angry, you first need to get in tune with your bodily reactions, emotions, and thoughts, as well as what you actually do when you become angry. Once you get a handle on these three factors, the changes you want to make can then be planned. The following exercise will help guide you through what happens when you become angry.

1.   After becoming angry, answer the following questions with a "YES" or "NO":

    a.   When I was angry, I noticed that my heart was pounding harder, faster, or louder. _____

    b.   When I was angry, I noticed my muscles felt tense or tight. _____

    c.   This was especially true for my (indicate the part of your body). _____

    _____

    d.   When I was angry, I noticed my skin felt hotter or became red. _____

    e.   When I was angry, I could feel the adrenaline rushing through my body.

    _____

    f.   When I become angry, I become overwhelmed with emotions. _____

    g.   Describe any other physiological reaction when you were angry.

    _____

    _____

    _____

2.   After becoming angry (or while angry), I was thinking:

_____

_____

_____

3.  When I was angry, I (describe what you did):

_____

_____

_____

4.  After I was angry I (describe what you did):

_____

_____

_____

5.  On a scale of 1 to 100, I would rate the level of my anger as: _____

6.  When I became angry, my family probably felt:

_____

_____

_____

7.  When I became angry, my family probably thought:

_____

_____

_____

# I DON'T HAVE ANY BRUISES BUT I STILL HURT

## GOALS OF THE EXERCISE

1. For family members to identify how they react to anger and conflict.
2. To help such family members feel validated and to affirm the thought that such behavior is inappropriate.

## ADDITIONAL HOMEWORK THAT MAY BE APPLICABLE TO ANGER PROBLEMS

- My Safe Place                                         Page 19
- What Am I Thinking When I Am Feeling Depressed?       Page 115
- Creating a Positive Outlook                           Page 227

## ADDITIONAL PROBLEMS FOR WHICH THIS EXERCISE MAY BE USEFUL

- Family Conflicts
- Verbal Abuse

## SUGGESTIONS FOR PROCESSING THIS EXERCISE WITH CLIENT

Verbal abuse can be as violent and as damaging as physical abuse. Many times, individuals attempt to minimize this damage with thoughts such as, "It's not like I am getting beat." The bruises left from verbal abuse are like scars on the soul. These bruises are internal, in that they get intertwined in how we create our sense of self. The following exercise is intended to help individuals verbalize that such experiences are unwanted and to assist them in learning how to assert themselves. It is intended for all family members who are the victims of such experiences.

# I DON'T HAVE ANY BRUISES BUT I STILL HURT

Verbal abuse can be as violent and damaging as physical abuse. Many times, you may try to minimize this with thoughts such as, "It's not like I am getting beat." However, the bruises left from verbal abuse are like scars on the soul. Sometimes these bruises hurt even more because these bruises are internal, in that they get intertwined in how we create our sense of self. The following exercise is intended to help you express that such experiences are unwanted and to assist you in learning how to assert yourself.

## FOR THE PERSON WHO DIRECTLY RECEIVES THE BRUNT OF VERBAL ABUSE

1.  When someone yells at me, calls me names, threatens me, or otherwise puts me down, I feel: _____

    _____

    _____

    _____

    _____

2.  The thoughts I have about myself when someone yells at me, calls me names, threatens me, or otherwise puts me down are:

    _____

    _____

    _____

    _____

    _____

    _____

3.  The thoughts I have about that person who is yelling at me, calling me names, threatening me, or otherwise putting me down are:

    _____

    _____

    _____

_____

_____

_____

4. The person who hurts me this way the most is: _____

5. Other people who have done this include:

_____

_____

_____

_____

_____

_____

6. What I want to say to this person (and these others) is:

_____

_____

_____

_____

_____

_____

_____

_____

7. Messages that I tell myself to make me feel better are:

_____

_____

_____

_____

_____

_____

_____

8. Things that I can do to make me feel better are:

_____

_____

_____

_____

_____

_____

_____

## FOR FAMILY MEMBERS WHO OBSERVE (SEE OR HEAR) ANOTHER FAMILY MEMBER BEING VERBALLY ABUSED

1.  The feelings I have when I observe someone in my family being yelled at, called names, threatened, or made to feel bad or scared are:

    _____

    _____

2.  The thoughts I have when such experiences occur are:

    _____

    _____

    _____

    _____

    _____

3.  The feelings I have regarding the person in my family who is doing the yelling, name-calling, threatening, and so forth are:

    _____

    _____

    _____

4.  The thoughts I have about the person in my family who is doing the yelling, name-calling, threatening, and so forth are:

    _____

    _____

    _____

    _____

5.  What I think should be done about this problem is:

    _____

    _____

_____
_____
_____
_____

6.  What I can say to _____ (person being verbally abused) to make him/her feel better is: _____

_____

_____

_____

_____

_____

_____

_____

# GO BLOW OUT SOME CANDLES

## GOALS OF THE EXERCISE

1.   To begin to develop control over your anger.
2.   To learn a way to relax more.

## ADDITIONAL HOMEWORK THAT MAY BE APPLICABLE TO ANGER PROBLEMS

- My Safe Place                                                        Page 19
- What Am I Thinking When I Am Feeling Depressed?        Page 115
- Creating a Positive Outlook                                    Page 227

## ADDITIONAL PROBLEMS FOR WHICH THIS EXERCISE MAY BE USEFUL

- Anxiety

## SUGGESTIONS FOR PROCESSING THIS EXERCISE WITH CLIENT

Because anger can be physically dangerous and can lead to the erosion of family life, it is important for individuals to learn how to redirect and reduce such feelings. Once individuals have learned some of the triggers to their anger as well as the physiological, cognitive, and behavioral responses to anger, it is important for them to learn how to redirect and prevent themselves from losing control. The following exercise is designed for any family member who wants to learn to take control over his/her anger.

# GO BLOW OUT SOME CANDLES

## FOR ANY FAMILY MEMBER WHO WANTS TO CONTROL HIS/HER ANGER

Practice the following exercise at least four times in the next week.

When feeling the initial signs of anger, practice taking a deep breath. To do so, breathe in through your nose. When you do, picture a balloon in your belly that you are trying to blow up. As you exhale through your mouth, count to 3. You can also picture blowing out a candle. Try to blow up 8 to 10 balloons, and blow out 8 to 10 candles.

# IT'S US AGAINST THE ANXIETY

## GOALS OF THE EXERCISE

1.  To increase non-anxious family members' understanding about anxiety.
2.  To increase ways non-anxious family members can be supportive.
3.  To reduce anxious family members' sense of isolation.

## ADDITIONAL HOMEWORK THAT MAY BE APPLICABLE TO ANXIETY

- My Safe Place                                      Page 19
- Acting as If                                       Page 52
- What Am I Thinking When I Am Depressed?            Page 115

## ADDITIONAL PROBLEMS IN WHICH THIS EXERCISE MAY BE USEFUL

- Depression
- Anger

## SUGGESTIONS FOR PROCESSING THIS EXERCISE WITH CLIENT

Anxiety can be quite debilitating. Oftentimes, it is our thought patterns that reinforce that feeling of dread. When we are anxious, we are frequently stuck in our heads worrying about something or someone. These thoughts of worry can be overpowering. Family members can try to be supportive but can too often become frustrated with the anxious family member. The anxious family member may then feel depressed and isolated. The following exercise is designed to help the non-anxious family members to become more understanding and in tune with what the anxious family member experiences in their heads. By doing this exercise as a family, the hope is that the anxious member may feel less isolated and more supported.

# IT'S US AGAINST THE ANXIETY

1. As a family unit, each member is to think of a time when they felt anxious. Each member is to write down this memory in as much detail as possible.

   a. I felt anxious when (describe when):

   _____

   _____

   b. I was with: _____

   c. We were (describe where you were):

   _____

   _____

2. In describing the situation take time for each family member to write out several anxious thoughts s/he may have had.

   _____

   _____

   _____

   _____

   _____

   _____

3. As a family, each member is to read aloud their situations and anxious thoughts.

4. Family should then brainstorm in order to generate calming, reassuring, encouraging types of thoughts to replace the anxious thoughts. (What else can I think about?)

5. Each family member can record the replacement thoughts on index cards, or a designated family member can record all of them on a sheet of paper for any member to review at any time.

# MY/OUR DAUGHTER IS AFRAID TO GO TO SCHOOL

## GOALS OF THE EXERCISE

1. Develop a basic understanding as to why the fear exists.
2. Develop alternative self-talk when feeling afraid to attend school.
3. Identify role of each family member in enabling or compounding the fears of the anxious child.

## ADDITIONAL HOMEWORK THAT MAY BE APPLICABLE TO ANXIETY PROBLEMS

- My Safe Place                                                  Page 19
- A Picture Is Worth a Thousand Words (just pictures 1–3)        Page 215
- Creating a Positive Outlook                                    Page 227

## ADDITIONAL PROBLEMS FOR WHICH THIS EXERCISE MAY BE USEFUL

- Low Self-Esteem[*]

## SUGGESTIONS FOR PROCESSING THIS EXERCISE WITH CLIENT

When a child is afraid of attending school, it is important to elicit what specific fears he/she has and why they may have developed. This can be accomplished directly in sessions (i.e., by Socratic questioning). Very often parents try to help a fearful child by giving him/her reassuring statements. However, very often this can actually maintain the anxiety. What is needed is for the child to develop self-assurance and some coping skills. To accomplish this, have the child list the various statements s/he makes when feeling frightened. Alongside of each fearful statement, have her/him write a reassuring or countering statement. Copy this or just the counterstatements on an index card. Whenever the child is feeling scared, direct her/him to take out the list and read it. These are referred to as coping cards. Whenever the child expresses fear to her/his parent(s), the parent(s) respond by saying, "Remember what you wrote on your coping card." Then have them rate the outcome of their response to the card (e.g., it helped some, a lot, did not help).

---

[*]This problem is not specifically discussed in detail in this volume.

# MY/OUR DAUGHTER IS AFRAID TO GO TO SCHOOL

## FOR PARENTS AND FEARFUL CHILD

Being a parent is the most difficult job in the world. When one of our children is hurting, our initial response is to take care of them, to fix the hurt. When that hurt is a fear of attending school, our natural response is to reassure our child that "everything will be fine" and "you are okay." This usually helps to some degree, but the anxiety returns once you stop the reassurance. To overcome this, your child/adolescent must learn to make self-reassuring statements. This allows them to take control. To accomplish this, have your child/adolescent list the various statements s/he makes when feeling frightened. Alongside of each fearful statement, have them write a reassuring or countering statement. Copy this or just the counterstatements on an index card. Whenever your child/adolescent is feeling scared, direct her/him to take out the list and read it to herself/himself. These are referred to as "coping cards." Whenever your child/adolescent expresses fear to you, respond by saying, "Remember what you wrote on your coping card."

| Fearful Self-Talk | Strong Self-Talk | Rate the Outcome |
|---|---|---|
| _____ | _____ | _____ |
| _____ | _____ | _____ |
| _____ | _____ | _____ |
| _____ | _____ | _____ |
| _____ | _____ | _____ |
| _____ | _____ | _____ |
| _____ | _____ | _____ |

# WHEN I FEEL ANXIOUS IT IS LIKE . . .

## GOALS OF THE EXERCISE

1. Help the anxious member identify times and situations when/where s/he feels anxious. Use physical examples as much as possible (e.g., butterflies in my stomach).
2. Have family understand the impact that anxiety has on the anxiety-ridden individual.
3. Anxious family member identifies automatic thoughts that accompany anxious feelings as well as the behavior that s/he engages in.
4. Anxious family member learns to practice cognitive restructuring techniques as well as behavioral rehearsal.
5. Family members learn to coach anxious family member in cognitive restructuring techniques and the use of new behaviors.

## ADDITIONAL HOMEWORK THAT MAY BE APPLICABLE TO ANXIETY PROBLEMS

- My Safe Place           Page 19
- A Picture Is Worth a Thousand Words (just pictures 1–3)     Page 215
- Creating a Positive Outlook      Page 227

## ADDITIONAL PROBLEMS FOR WHICH THIS EXERCISE MAY BE USEFUL

- Anger
- Depression

## SUGGESTIONS FOR PROCESSING THIS EXERCISE WITH CLIENT

When a person feels anxious, one of their main concerns is a fear of losing control. By helping them identify when and in what situations they feel anxious, as well as what they think about and what they do when anxious, you can help them regain a sense of control. It is also important for you to help the other family members who are struggling with feelings of frustration and helplessness over dealing with the anxious family member. Teaching the other family members ways to be helpful and effectively supportive will help in changing how the family as a unit interacts with the anxious member.

# WHEN I FEEL ANXIOUS IT IS LIKE . . .

If you are feeling anxious, you most likely want to learn ways to regain control and overcome that fear of losing control. Figuring out the cues or situations in which you tend to feel anxious, as well as what goes through your mind and what you do in those circumstances will give you and your therapist a better understanding of what you need to do differently.

## FOR THE ANXIOUS FAMILY MEMBER

Over the next week identify the times/situations, your thoughts/images, emotions, and behaviors when experiencing anxiety.

1.  I felt anxious when:

    _____

    _____

    _____

    a.  Describe what went through your mind (e.g., thoughts, images) when you were feeling anxious. _____

    _____

    _____

    b.  Describe what you did when you were feeling anxious.

    _____

    _____

    _____

2.  I felt anxious when:

    _____

    _____

    _____

    a.   Describe what went through your mind (e.g., thoughts, images) when you were feeling anxious. _____

_____

_____

    b.   Describe what you did when you were feeling anxious.

_____

_____

_____

3.    I felt anxious when:

_____

_____

_____

    a.   Describe what went through your mind (e.g., thoughts, images) when you were feeling anxious. _____

_____

_____

    b.   Describe what you did when you were feeling anxious.

_____

_____

_____

4.    I felt anxious when:

_____

_____

_____

    a.   Describe what went through your mind (e.g., thoughts, images) when you were feeling anxious. _____

_____

_____

    b.   Describe what you did when you were feeling anxious.

_____

_____

_____

Share this with the other family members.

# MY MOTHER'S ANXIETY MAKES ME FEEL. . .

## GOALS OF THE EXERCISE

1. Have family members identify what it is like for them when their parent(s) is/are anxious.
2. Have family members express their feelings regarding living with an anxiety-ridden person.

## ADDITIONAL HOMEWORK THAT MAY BE APPLICABLE TO ANXIETY PROBLEMS

- My Safe Place         Page 19
- A Picture Is Worth a Thousand Words (just pictures 1–3)      Page 215
- Creating a Positive Outlook        Page 227

## ADDITIONAL PROBLEMS FOR WHICH THIS EXERCISE MAY BE USEFUL

- Anger Problems
- Depression

## SUGGESTIONS FOR PROCESSING THIS EXERCISE WITH CLIENT

Very often family members are not given a forum to discuss their own thoughts and feelings regarding what it is like for them to live with someone who is frequently anxious. The following exercise is intended to create such a forum.

# MY MOTHER'S ANXIETY MAKES ME FEEL . . .

## FOR FAMILY MEMBERS

Identify two or three situations in which you observed your parent or spouse being anxious, and then describe how you knew that s/he was anxious.

1.  I remember when _____ was _____

    _____

    _____

    a.  I could tell _____ was anxious because _____

    _____

    _____

    b.  I began thinking and feeling _____

    _____

    _____

2.  I remember when _____ was _____

    _____

    _____

    a.  I could tell _____ was anxious because _____

    _____

    _____

    b.  I began thinking and feeling _____

    _____

    _____

3.  I remember when _____ was _____

    _____

    _____

    a.  I could tell _____ was anxious because _____

    _____

    _____

   b.  I began thinking and feeling _____

_____

_____

4.  I remember when _____ was _____

_____

_____

   a.  I could tell _____ was anxious because _____

_____

_____

   b.  I began thinking and feeling _____

_____

_____

5.  I remember when _____ was _____

_____

_____

   a.  I could tell _____ was anxious because _____

_____

_____

   b.  I began thinking and feeling _____

_____

_____

6.  I remember when _____ was _____

_____

_____

   a.  I could tell _____ was anxious because _____

_____

_____

   b.  I began thinking and feeling _____

_____

_____

# MY CHILD JUST WON'T LISTEN

## GOALS OF THE EXERCISE

1. For parents and children to develop more cooperation with each other.
2. Decrease the amount of conflict and tension within the home/family.
3. Identify the expectations that parents have of their children and that children have of their parents.

## ADDITIONAL HOMEWORK THAT MAY BE APPLICABLE TO BEHAVIORAL PROBLEMS IN CHILDREN AND ADOLESCENTS

- My Safe Place                                                    Page 19
- A Picture Is Worth a Thousand Words (just pictures 1–3)          Page 215
- What Do Others Value about Me?                                   Page 117
- My Teenager Is Truant                                            Page 194
- Creating a Positive Outlook                                      Page 227

## ADDITIONAL PROBLEMS FOR WHICH THIS EXERCISE MAY BE USEFUL

- Anger
- Depression
- Substance Abuse

## SUGGESTIONS FOR PROCESSING THIS EXERCISE WITH CLIENT

Oftentimes, a child who frequently disobeys and doesn't listen creates and induces anger/frustration and resentment in his/her parent. Such situations frequently lead to or end in arguments and yelling matches. The following exercise is designed to assist families in developing a sense of control by identifying their view of the conflicts, their thoughts and feelings about the conflicts, and how they would like things to be.

# MY CHILD JUST WON'T LISTEN

## FOR CHILD AND PARENTS

The following exercise is designed for each of you to regain a sense of control and stabilization within the family. Find a quiet time to think about each of the questions below. Try to be as objective and specific as you can.

1. What do you hate most about the conflicts with your child/parent?

   _____

   _____

   _____

   _____

   _____

   _____

2. When do these conflicts tend to happen?

   _____

   _____

   _____

   _____

   _____

   _____

3. What do you try to do to limit or decrease the conflicts?

   _____

   _____

   _____

   _____

   _____

   _____

4.  What does your parent/child do to limit or decrease the conflicts?

    _____
    _____
    _____
    _____
    _____
    _____

5.  What else could your parent/child do to limit or decrease the conflicts?

    _____
    _____
    _____
    _____
    _____
    _____

6.  Describe a time in which you were getting along with your child/parent. What were you doing, and what were they doing?

    _____
    _____
    _____
    _____
    _____
    _____

7.  How did this make you feel?

    _____
    _____
    _____

8.  How hard would it be for you to act the way you described yourself in #6 on a regular basis?

    _____
    _____
    _____

    _____  That would be easy.
    _____  That would be a little hard.
    _____  That would be pretty hard.
    _____  That would be next to impossible.

9. How would life be if you could act that way more days than not?

_____

_____

_____

_____

# ACTING AS IF

## GOALS OF THE EXERCISE

1. To identify the rules or guidelines for living together as a family.
2. To identify the expectations parents have of their child/adolescent and that the child/adolescent has of his/her parents.
3. To decrease the amount of conflict in the home/family.

## ADDITIONAL HOMEWORK THAT MAY BE APPLICABLE TO BEHAVIORAL PROBLEMS IN CHILDREN AND ADOLESCENTS

- My Safe Place                                                     Page 19
- A Picture Is Worth a Thousand Words (just pictures 1–3)           Page 215
- What Do Others Value about Me?                                    Page 117
- My Teenager Is Truant                                             Page 194
- Creating a Positive Outlook                                       Page 227

## ADDITIONAL PROBLEMS FOR WHICH THIS EXERCISE MAY BE USEFUL

- Depression
- Family Conflicts

## SUGGESTIONS FOR PROCESSING THIS EXERCISE WITH CLIENT

Family members in general are able to easily describe the problems between them. It is important to identify such concerns—but it is equally important to describe how family members would want to interact and get along. Once they do so, the therapist should encourage them to put their description into action even if they are just acting.

# ACTING AS IF

## FOR FAMILY MEMBERS EXPERIENCING CONFLICT

In most families, it is much easier to describe and focus on the problems. Too often families become caught up with how bad things are and get stuck in a pattern or cycle of behaving in a certain way. The following exercise is designed to help you identify problem behavior that your family is experiencing, and more important, to help you to get a clearer picture of how each of you would like to act as a family. By identifying how each of you would like to be as a family, you take charge of directing and creating a new pattern or cycle as a family.

1. List the problem behaviors, and be as specific as you can.

   _____
   _____
   _____
   _____
   _____
   _____
   _____
   _____
   _____

2. When do these behaviors typically occur? Try to describe the situation.

   _____
   _____
   _____
   _____
   _____

3. Describe what your parent, child, or adolescent does that tends to make the situation worse. _____

   _____
   _____

_____

_____

_____

_____

_____

4.   Describe what you do that tends to make the situation worse.

_____

_____

_____

_____

_____

5.   Describe an ideal time. How would everyone act if you were all getting along?

_____

_____

_____

_____

6.   As a family, pick one day this week in which all of you will plan to act as described in #5 above. Write in the agreed-upon date. _____

7.   Describe your thoughts and feelings when everyone acted this way.

_____

_____

_____

_____

25

# WE HAVE TO MAKE SOME TYPE OF AGREEMENT

## GOALS OF THE EXERCISE

1.  To identify the problematic behaviors.
2.  To identify the rewards and consequences of behaviors.
3.  To help families focus on specific areas of change.
4.  To help parents work together consistently.
5.  For children or adolescents to know what is expected.

## ADDITIONAL HOMEWORK THAT MAY BE APPLICABLE TO BEHAVIORAL PROBLEMS IN CHILDREN AND ADOLESCENTS

## ADDITIONAL PROBLEMS FOR WHICH THIS EXERCISE MAY BE USEFUL

- Communication Problems
- Family Conflicts

## SUGGESTIONS FOR PROCESSING THIS EXERCISE WITH CLIENT

Sometimes families become overwhelmed with the amount of conflict and tension in the home. It is important to help them zero in on two or three specific areas of change. This allows them to see progress more clearly and is more realistic than trying to change the world all at once.

# WE HAVE TO MAKE SOME KIND OF AGREEMENT

## FOR PARENTS OF CHILD/ADOLESCENT EXPERIENCING PROBLEMATIC BEHAVIORS

The following exercise is designed to help you reduce the feelings of frustration and being overwhelmed with the "problems" in the family. Identifying two or three specific areas that you want to change allows you to become more focused and keep things more manageable. This will also help you to see progress more clearly.

1. List the problem behaviors, and be as specific as you can. Number each one individually. _____

   _____

   _____

   _____

   _____

   _____

   _____

   _____

   _____

   _____

2. For each numbered behavior above, describe what you expect instead of what you are getting (e.g., polite language in a normal tone of voice versus cursing whenever he/she is in the house). _____

   _____

   _____

   _____

   _____

   _____

   _____

_____

_____

_____

3.  List what your child/adolescent views as a reward (e.g., talking on the phone, going outside, using the car, having friends over).

    _____

    _____

    _____

    _____

    _____

    _____

    _____

4.  List what your child/adolescent views as a consequence.

    _____

    _____

    _____

    _____

    _____

    _____

    _____

5.  Pick two or three of the expected behaviors that you want to see more frequently.

    _____

    _____

    _____

    _____

6.  Inform your child/adolescent that each day you will be looking to see that s/he is demonstrating such behavior. Each day that you see evidence of their behavior, record and date exactly what it is that you observe. Review it with your spouse/partner, and then review it with your son/daughter. Explain the concept that evidence equals rewards.

7.  Parents are to speak calmly, but in a matter-of-fact tone of voice to their child/adolescent when reviewing such evidence.

# CHARTING OUR COURSE

## GOALS OF THE EXERCISE

1. For younger children to visualize their progress.
2. For parents to visualize their child's progress and help him/her stay focused and consistent.

## ADDITIONAL HOMEWORK THAT MAY BE APPLICABLE TO BEHAVIORAL PROBLEMS IN CHILDREN AND ADOLESCENTS

## ADDITIONAL PROBLEMS FOR WHICH THIS EXERCISE MAY BE USEFUL

- Pervasive Developmental Disorder

## SUGGESTIONS FOR PROCESSING THIS EXERCISE WITH CLIENT

For younger children, charting expected behavior is very helpful. Using a chart or graph of some type allows them to visualize how well they are doing. Such visual aids are also helpful for parents to notice the positives in their child. This can be a challenge when families are overly focused on the "problems." The exercise that follows is designed to shift some of the focus onto the positive and to shape more of the expected/desired behavior in children.

# CHARTING OUR COURSE

## FOR PARENTS AND CHILD

This exercise is designed especially for younger children. Oftentimes a child prefers to "see" that s/he is doing well. Having a visual aid such as a chart also helps you as the parent to "see" more of the positives that your son or daughter is doing.

1.  Identify three behaviors that you would like to see more frequently with your child (e.g., instead of not talking back we want Johnny to listen by the second or third prompt). _____

    _____

    _____

2.  Identify two behaviors that are not a problem. These can be behaviors that your child does without much (if any) prodding (e.g., gets dressed by himself/herself).

    _____

    _____

3.  With your child, identify three or four rewarding behaviors (e.g., watching TV for 30 minutes; riding a bike; special time with Mom and/or Dad, such as playing a board game or reading a book together).

    _____

    _____

    _____

    _____

4.  Put the list of rewards on a separate sheet of paper.

5.  Use the following chart to fill in the information in the column for behavior as identified in items 1 and 2 above.

| Behavior | Sun. | Mon. | Tues. | Wed. | Thurs. | Fri. | Sat. |
|----------|------|------|-------|------|--------|------|------|
|          |      |      |       |      |        |      |      |
|          |      |      |       |      |        |      |      |
|          |      |      |       |      |        |      |      |
|          |      |      |       |      |        |      |      |
| Totals   |      |      |       |      |        |      |      |

6.  Each day, or evening, sit with your child and review the day. For each desired behavior displayed, a sticker, checkmark, or smiley face should be entered into the corresponding block on the chart.

7.  The bottom row is used for adding up the number of stickers, checkmarks, or smiley faces.

8.  The total number of desired behaviors for each day or for each week can be traded in for rewards identified in item 4.

# MY MOM JUST WON'T STAY ON HER MEDICATION

## GOALS FOR THIS EXERCISE

1. Increase the consistency of medication adherence.
2. Family members develop an understanding of how they can be supportive.

## ADDITIONAL HOMEWORK THAT MAY BE APPLICABLE TO BIPOLAR DISORDER

- My Safe Place                                            Page 19
- What Am I Thinking When I Am Feeling Depressed?          Page 115

## ADDITIONAL PROBLEMS FOR WHICH THIS EXERCISE MAY BE USEFUL

- Anxiety
- Depression

## SUGGESTIONS FOR PROCESSING THIS EXERCISE WITH CLIENT

The most frequent treatment for a person with bipolar disorder is medication. This, however, is frequently the most difficult part of the treatment. Individuals with bipolar disorder oftentimes do not want to stop feeling the energy and excitement they experience during a manic phase. As a result, helping them to consistently take their medication can be a challenge.

# MY MOM JUST WON'T STAY ON HER MEDICATION

Having to continuously take medication can become very frustrating. Many times, you probably wish you could just stop—and perhaps you do stop. The following exercise is designed to help you and your family to identify and express some of their thoughts and feelings regarding medication compliance.

## FOR THE FAMILY MEMBER WHO NEEDS TO TAKE MEDICATION

1.  Describe your thoughts and feelings about having to take medication.

    _____

    _____

    _____

    _____

    _____

2.  Describe your thoughts and feelings when you want to discontinue taking your medication. What is going on in your life during such times?

    _____

    _____

    _____

    _____

    _____

3.  Give some reasons why it is okay to stop taking your medication.

    _____

    _____

    _____

    _____

    _____

4. Give some reasons why it is not okay to stop taking your medication.

   _____

   _____

   _____

   _____

   _____

5. Describe how you feel after not taking your medication for a few days, a week, or a month. _____

   _____

   _____

   _____

6. How is your relationship with family members affected when you do not take your medication on a consistent basis?

   _____

   _____

   _____

   _____

7. Describe how this makes you feel.

   _____

   _____

   _____

8. Describe how your family responds to you when you take your medication on a consistent basis. _____

   _____

   _____

   _____

9. Describe how this makes you feel.

   _____

   _____

   _____

## FOR FAMILY MEMBERS

1. Describe how your _____ acts when s/he is taking her/his medication regularly. _____

   _____

   _____

   _____

2. How does this make you feel?

   _____

   _____

   _____

3. Describe how you tend to act toward _____ during such times.

   _____

   _____

   _____

   _____

4. Describe how your _____ acts when s/he is not taking her/his medication regularly. _____

   _____

   _____

   _____

5. How does this make you feel?

   _____

   _____

   _____

6. Describe how you react to your _____ when s/he is not taking her/his medication. _____

   _____

   _____

   _____

7. Does this help the situation or make it worse? Describe.

   _____

   _____

   _____

8.  Ask your _____ how you could be a support to him/her. Record the response here. _____

_____

_____

_____

# WHAT DO I SAY? WHAT CAN I SAY?

## GOALS OF THE EXERCISE

1. To increase awareness of blaming comments.
2. To identify alternatives to blaming comments.
3. To reduce frequency of blaming interactions.

## ADDITIONAL HOMEWORK THAT MAY BE APPLICABLE TO BLAME

- I Gotta Stop Thinking This Way                        Page 213
- What Am I Thinking When I Am Feeling Depressed?        Page 115
- Creating a Positive Outlook                           Page 227

## ADDITIONAL PROBLEMS IN WHICH THIS EXERCISE MAY BE USEFUL

- Anger Management
- Anxiety
- Communication Problems
- Depression

## SUGGESTIONS FOR PROCESSING THIS EXERCISE WITH CLIENT

When families come for treatment, the behavioral patterns they display have typically been in place for a long time. Individuals who tend to blame others are often not aware of their own behavior in the moment. It may almost be similar to a knee jerk reaction or automatic response. In order to change such an ingrained behavior, individuals need to initially increase their awareness of such behavior and also learn to practice alternative behaviors.

# WHAT DO I SAY? WHAT CAN I SAY?

This exercise is designed to help the individual who struggles to catch, interrupt, and change his or her blaming behavior. It is important that the individual acknowledge a desire to change his or her blaming behavior and recognize that blaming causes emotional pain within the family. The family will also need to acknowledge a willingness to put aside their anger/frustration. To aid in this process, the family can make a formal commitment by signing the agreement below.

For the person struggling with blaming:

I _____ acknowledge that I struggle with blaming and want that to change. I understand that blaming hurts my family, and I don't want to hurt my family. I realize I need to become more aware of how frequently I do this. I also acknowledge that to change this behavior I will need the help of my family.

_____        Date: _____

For each family member:

I _____, _____, _____, _____, _____, _____, agree to put aside any anger/frustration I have because I want things to change. I know it is hard to trust this process, and I agree to do my part.

_____        Date: _____

_____        Date: _____

_____        Date: _____

_____        Date: _____

_____        Date: _____

_____        Date: _____

In order to increase one's awareness of blaming, you will require the help of family members. Therefore, as a family, each member is to track blaming comments made for a week or two. This can be done by recording comments on a note and dropping it in a jar (see The Blaming Jar homework). It is important, although rather difficult, to avoid acting in a negative fashion or being angry toward the person who makes the blaming comment. This will only increase the conflict.

In order to increase one's awareness of such situations, the family will need to point out such comments when they occur. It is also fine, even preferable for the individual who makes the blaming comment to identify this behavior in him/herself.

After collecting the "blaming comments" for a week or two, the family should come together to brainstorm alternative statements to the blaming behavior. This can be accomplished by listing the blaming statements on one side of a paper and subsequently recording alternative statements on the other side. The family should be encouraged to use "I" messages. These alternative messages should also avoid aggressive or degrading comments.

Use the following chart as a way of identifying alternatives to blaming comments.

| Blaming Comments | Alternative Comments |
|---|---|
|  |  |
|  |  |
|  |  |
|  |  |
|  |  |
|  |  |
|  |  |
|  |  |

The family member who made the blaming comments should practice making the alternative comments while addressing the person s/he blamed originally.

For the next week or two, the family should track the times that alternative comments to blaming were made. These situations should also be acknowledged by the family as a whole as a way to reinforce this new behavior.

# DON'T LOOK AT ME, ASK HIM

## GOALS OF THE EXERCISE

1. For family members to take responsibility for their words and actions.
2. To reduce the frequency and intensity of blaming situations.
3. To encourage positive interactions.

## ADDITIONAL HOMEWORK THAT MAY BE APPLICABLE TO BLAMING

- What Am I Thinking When I Am Feeling Depressed?    Page 115
- Creating a Positive Outlook    Page 227

## ADDITIONAL PROBLEMS FOR WHICH THIS EXERCISE MAY BE USEFUL

- Anger

## SUGGESTIONS FOR PROCESSING THIS EXERCISE WITH THE CLIENT

The following exercise is designed to help individuals take note of their own behaviors (i.e., when they engage in blaming others). By increasing self-monitoring, individuals are more likely to reduce negative behaviors. Individuals are also more likely to begin to develop a sense of empathy for those they hurt.

# DON'T LOOK AT ME, ASK HIM

## FOR ALL FAMILY MEMBERS

Each family member is to write two letters (e.g., Dear Jane). In the first letter, describe your thoughts and feelings regarding why you were blaming or pointing a finger at someone else. In the second letter, describe some of the thoughts and feelings of the person you are blaming.

1.  The first letter is to justify why the individual who is blaming is upset and pointing a finger at someone else. This letter must use "I" statements such as "I feel angry when I can't find my things." In describing what happened, "I" statements must also be used. For example, "I looked all around the house and could not find my _____. That's when I saw _____ sitting in the chair with what I perceived as a smirk on his/her face. It made me think that he/she was laughing at me."

2.  The second letter is to write why the other person (who was being blamed) should feel upset. This letter must be crafted similar to an attorney arguing his/her client's case. This letter is to focus solely on how the person who was being blamed feels, thinks, and perceives the situation. For example, "He was watching me run around the house, screaming, yelling, and looking for a pen. It was not his pen and he did tell me to use another pen. He was busy trying to complete his own work. He felt angry that I was accusing him of something even though there was no proof."

# THE BLAMING JAR

## GOALS OF THE EXERCISE

1. To increase the level of self-monitoring for the individuals who are engaging in blaming others.
2. To decrease the amount of blaming others.

## ADDITIONAL HOMEWORK THAT MAY BE APPLICABLE TO BLAMING PROBLEMS

- What Am I Thinking When I Am Feeling Depressed?          Page 115
- Creating a Positive Outlook          Page 227

## ADDITIONAL PROBLEMS FOR WHICH THIS EXERCISE MAY BE USEFUL

- Behavioral Problems (e.g., "Cursing Jar")

## SUGGESTIONS FOR PROCESSING THIS EXERCISE WITH THE CLIENT

The "Blaming Jar" can be used to decrease almost any undesired behavior (e.g., cursing, being late). The objective is to hold the person accountable for the undesired behavior. Using the Blaming Jar within a family setting increases the likelihood of a person being held accountable because of the additional people watching.

# THE BLAMING JAR

## FOR ALL FAMILY MEMBERS

This exercise can be in place for several weeks. In fact, it is better to have all family members agree to a three- or four-week contract. During this time, any individual who blames someone else without proof of his/her statements must place either a quarter or a dollar in the jar. At the end of the three or four weeks, the money is used to treat the family (e.g., renting a video which all can watch, buying everyone ice cream).

For younger children or those who are not earning any money, instead of putting a quarter/dollar in the jar, they are to write their name and that of the person they were blaming on a piece of paper and put that into the jar. Each week, these individuals are to do something nice for the person they blamed (e.g., help with an older brother or sisters' chore).

# WHAT'S MY JOB?

## GOALS OF THE EXERCISE

1.  To evenly divide the household responsibilities among all family members.
2.  To clearly define each person's responsibility.

## ADDITIONAL HOMEWORK THAT MAY BE APPLICABLE TO BLAMING PROBLEMS

- What Am I Thinking When I Am Feeling Depressed?          Page 115
- Creating a Positive Outlook                              Page 227

## ADDITIONAL PROBLEMS FOR WHICH THIS EXERCISE MAY BE USEFUL

- Behavioral Problems
- Communication Problems

## SUGGESTIONS FOR PROCESSING THIS EXERCISE WITH THE CLIENT

Many times family members complain about other members not helping out around the house. The following exercise is designed to help families reduce chores into specific duties or responsibilities for each person.

# WHAT'S MY JOB?

## FOR ALL FAMILY MEMBERS

Family members are to identify the basic household responsibilities and the individual family members who are to perform them (e.g., who takes out the trash and when, who feeds the cat and when, who puts the kids to bed and when, who does what yard work and when). This information can be put into a chart similar to the example provided here or simply listed on the calendar. It should then be displayed in an area where all family members can easily view it. The best place is usually in the kitchen.

| | **Household Responsibilities** | **Family Member** |
|---|---|---|
| 1. | _____ | _____ |
| 2. | _____ | _____ |
| 3. | _____ | _____ |
| 4. | _____ | _____ |
| 5. | _____ | _____ |
| 6. | _____ | _____ |
| 7. | _____ | _____ |
| 8. | _____ | _____ |
| 9. | _____ | _____ |
| 10. | _____ | _____ |

## Family Chore Chart

| Sun. | | Mon. | | Tues. | | Wed. | | Thurs. | |
|---|---|---|---|---|---|---|---|---|---|
| Name | Chore | Name | Chore | Name | Chore | Name | Chore | Name | Chore |
| | | | | | | | | | |
| | | | | | | | | | |
| | | | | | | | | | |
| | | | | | | | | | |
| | | | | | | | | | |
| | | | | | | | | | |
| | | | | | | | | | |
| | | | | | | | | | |

# I DON'T LIKE IT WHEN YOU . . .

## GOALS OF THE EXERCISE

1. For all family members, especially the children, to be able to express their negative feelings about any unfairness they perceive or experience.
2. To help family members listen to and hear the concerns of other family members.
3. To identify and agree on changes that are needed to create an atmosphere of safety and coherence.

## ADDITIONAL HOMEWORK THAT MAY BE APPLICABLE TO BLENDED FAMILIES

- My Safe Place                                      Page 19
- A Picture Is Worth a Thousand Words                Page 215
- How Can I Talk So He'll Listen?                     Page 89

## ADDITIONAL PROBLEMS FOR WHICH THIS EXERCISE MAY BE USEFUL

- Communication Problems
- Lack of Assertiveness
- Separation/Divorce

## SUGGESTIONS FOR PROCESSING THIS EXERCISE WITH THE CLIENT

Blended families experience a range of emotions and often struggle with being able to express such feelings. Sometimes individuals, especially children, find it helpful to have an outline that guides them through the process of identifying and expressing their feelings. This exercise is intended to create that guideline and will help them find the words to express their feelings. The exercise is also geared toward helping individuals listen to and hear feedback, which is often just as difficult as being able to express your feelings. When family members return with their homework, it is important that the family feel safe in expressing their feelings. If you do not feel a family member is able to listen to the feedback without becoming defensive, this exercise should not be completed with that member present. That member should be referred for individual sessions to teach him or her how to listen openly and be able to regulate and manage his or her emotional reaction.

# I DON'T LIKE IT WHEN YOU . . .

All family members can use this exercise.

Over the next two weeks, each family member should have a copy of the following sentence stems. During this time, each member is to record times they felt upset in some way regarding the family interactions. For younger children, an older sibling or parent may need to help them out with this. When a younger child is visibly upset, take time to write down what s/he is upset about and ask the child to describe their thoughts and feelings. The person helping should not be the person the child is upset with.

Today's date and time: _____

Setting: (e.g., living room, kitchen) _____

I was upset with: _____

S/he (describe what s/he did or didn't do, said or didn't say):

_____
_____
_____
_____

This made me feel:

_____
_____

I wish s/he would have (describe what you would have want the other person to have done instead):

_____
_____
_____
_____

For younger children, once this is completed have them repeat verbally what was written. This will give them a chance to practice asserting themselves in an appropriate way.

Today's date and time: _____

Setting: (e.g., living room, kitchen): _____

I was upset with: _____

S/he (describe what s/he did or didn't do, said or didn't say):

_____

_____

_____

_____

This made me feel:

_____

_____

I wish s/he would have (describe what you would have want the other person to have done instead):

_____

_____

_____

_____

For younger children, once this is completed have them repeat verbally what was written. This will give them a chance to practice asserting themselves in an appropriate manner.

Today's date and time: _____

Setting: (e.g., living room, kitchen) _____

I was upset with: _____

S/he (describe what s/he did or didn't do, said or didn't say):

_____

_____

_____

_____

This made me feel:

_____

_____

I wish s/he would have (describe what you would have want the other person to have done instead):

_____

_____

_____

_____

For younger children, once this is completed have them repeat verbally what was written. This will give them a chance to practice asserting themselves in an appropriate way.

Each family member should bring this homework assignment with them to the family session. Before reading them, all family members should give a verbal agreement to actively listen and NOT respond in an attacking or defensive manner.

# I HAVE TOO MANY PARENTS

## GOALS OF THE EXERCISE

1. Family members accept responsibility for the adjustment that comes with joining a new family.
2. Family members agree to make exceptions in order to live together harmoniously.
3. Family members explore some of the myths about blended families.

## ADDITIONAL HOMEWORK THAT MAY BE APPLICABLE TO BLENDED FAMILIES

- My Safe Place                                                    Page 19
- A Picture Is Worth a Thousand Words (just pictures 1–3)          Page 215
- Creating a Positive Outlook                                      Page 227

## ADDITIONAL PROBLEMS FOR WHICH THIS EXERCISE MAY BE USEFUL

- Adoption

## SUGGESTIONS FOR PROCESSING THIS EXERCISE WITH THE CLIENT

Among the most common reactions to blended families are feelings of resentment and the issue of acceptance. It is important for family members to feel that they can express such feelings and thoughts freely. But these are usually difficult for parents to hear and sometimes difficult for children/adolescents to articulate. The following exercise is designed for an existing blended family that needs to commence with this process. This can also be used for a family that is in transition and is about to become a blended family.

# I HAVE TOO MANY PARENTS

## FOR FAMILY MEMBERS IN A NEW BLENDED FAMILY

Whether one of your parents has already remarried or is about to remarry, it is important for you to be able to express your thoughts and feelings regarding this matter. The following exercise will help you in expressing such thoughts and feelings.

Answer the questions that follow as best you can.

1. What are your thoughts and feelings about each family member (natural/step/foster/adoptive)? _____

    _____

    _____

    _____

    _____

2. Identify one or two situations or events (for each member) that influenced you to feel the way that you do.

    _____

    _____

    _____

    _____

    _____

    _____

    _____

    _____

    _____

3. What do you believe their feelings are about you?

    _____

    _____

    _____

    _____

_____

_____

4. Identify one or two situations or times that made you think in such a way. (Do this for each family member.)

_____

_____

_____

_____

_____

_____

_____

_____

_____

5. How did you learn that you were going to have another family?

_____

_____

_____

_____

_____

_____

_____

6. What was your worst fear about becoming part of a blended family?

_____

_____

_____

_____

_____

7. What is it about this entire issue that makes you uneasy? Angry? Sad? Happy? Scared? _____

_____

_____

_____

_____

_____

_____

_____

8. What does it mean to you to have "stepfamily" members?

_____

_____

_____

_____

_____

9. What does this mean for your biological or "natural" family?

_____

_____

_____

_____

_____

10. What do you do to make it difficult to get along as a stepfamily unit?

_____

_____

_____

_____

_____

11. Identify at least two behaviors that you can do to make things better. List some pros and cons to doing this.

_____

_____

_____

_____

_____

_____

12. Share your responses to this exercise in your next family session.

# WE NEED TO AGREE

## GOALS OF THE EXERCISE

1. All parents (step, biological, foster, and adoptive) agree to cooperate and work together in the best interest of the children.
2. Children feel greater security and a sense of stability.

## ADDITIONAL HOMEWORK THAT MAY BE APPLICABLE TO BLENDED FAMILIES

* My Safe Place                                                           Page 19
* Creating a Positive Outlook                                             Page 227
* A Picture Is Worth a Thousand Words (just pictures 1–3)                 Page 215

## ADDITIONAL PROBLEMS FOR WHICH THIS EXERCISE MAY BE USEFUL

* Adoption

## SUGGESTIONS FOR PROCESSING THIS EXERCISE WITH CLIENT

Another common difficulty is for divorced parents to continue acting as a unified team. It is sometimes beneficial to have a session with the parents (including stepparents) to identify and discuss parenting differences. Although this is no easy task, it is suggested that you create a contract that everyone signs in order to reinforce the commitment to getting along. You may want to include the following areas:

1. Visitation schedule
2. Standard house rules
3. Expectations regarding schoolwork
4. Expectations regarding behaviors

# WE NEED TO AGREE

## FOR PARENTS IN A DIVORCED OR REMARRIED FAMILY

Being in a divorced or remarried family can be difficult for lots of reasons. You can reduce the difficulties by working together. As parents, it is especially important for you to both be on the same page with each other. Regardless of whether you are married to each other or not, you are both still parents to your children. One of the ways you can make things easier on yourself as well as on the rest of the family is to work together. You are probably saying, "If we could do that we wouldn't have gotten divorced!" You are right. But sometimes it can actually be easier to work together when you are no longer married to or living with each other. The following exercise is designed to help you start the process of working together to reduce your own level of stress (as well as everyone else's).

1.  Complete the following schedule for visitation.

|  | Sunday | Monday | Tuesday | Wednesday | Thursday | Friday | Saturday |
|---|---|---|---|---|---|---|---|
| Pick-Up Time |  |  |  |  |  |  |  |
| Drop-Off Time |  |  |  |  |  |  |  |

Once you have agreed on this schedule, give a copy to each child and keep one for yourself.

2.  Identify house rules (e.g., dinner is at 6:00 P.M.; curfew is at 9:00 P.M.; and homework is to be done before you go outside or have friends over). The more that your house rules match up with your ex-spouse's, the more consistency (and less confusion) there is for your children. A copy of the house rules should then be given to each child (and keep one for yourself).

## Dad's House Rules

1. _____
2. _____
3. _____
4. _____
5. _____
6. _____
7. _____

## Mom's House Rules

1. _____
2. _____
3. _____
4. _____
5. _____
6. _____
7. _____

Ideally, these two lists can be traded in for one list labeled "Parents' House Rules."

3. Describe your expectations for school (e.g., You need to maintain at least a "C" average in all of your subjects; homework is to be done before any social activities). Your children should also be able to voice their input to this. Each child should have his or her own list of expectations.

## Dad's Expectations for School

1. _____
2. _____
3. _____
4. _____
5. _____

## Mom's Expectations for School

1. _____
2. _____
3. _____
4. _____
5. _____

Ideally, these two lists can be traded in for one list labeled "Parents' Expectations for School."

4. Describe the type of behavior you expect of each other (this includes parents with kids as well as kids with parents). For example, "When we speak to each other, we are to speak calmly and with an inside voice and without any cursing or name-calling."

**Dad's Expectations of How We Should Treat Each Other**

1. _____
2. _____
3. _____
4. _____
5. _____
6. _____
7. _____

**Mom's Expectations of How We Should Treat Each Other**

1. _____
2. _____
3. _____
4. _____
5. _____
6. _____
7. _____

Ideally, these two lists can be traded in for one list labeled "Parents' Expectations of How We Should Treat Each Other."

# HOW CAN I TALK SO HE'LL LISTEN?

## GOALS OF THE EXERCISE

1.  To learn effective ways of communicating.
2.  To feel acknowledged and heard.
3.  To improve assertiveness and be able to convey your true thoughts and feelings.

## ADDITIONAL HOMEWORK THAT MAY BE APPLICABLE TO COMMUNICATION PROBLEMS

- What Am I Thinking When I Am Feeling Depressed?        Page 115
- Why Can't You Understand My Side for Once?        Pages 164, 166

## ADDITIONAL PROBLEMS IN WHICH THIS EXERCISE MAY BE USEFUL

- Family Conflict*

## SUGGESTIONS FOR PROCESSING THIS EXERCISE WITH THE CLIENT

It is very common in families experiencing conflict to have difficulties with communication. Members frequently report that they feel dismissed, unheard, and misunderstood. Unfortunately, there are not many places where people learn how to effectively communicate with each other. All of us are pretty much left to our experiences with others and watching how our parents, siblings, relatives, teachers, and friends communicate. A primary problem people have in communicating effectively is difficulties with listening. The following exercise is designed to help people learn in a step-by-step fashion how to listen actively and effectively as well as express their thoughts and feelings clearly and directly.

---

*This problem is not specifically discussed in detail in this volume.

# HOW CAN I TALK SO HE'LL LISTEN?

## FOR ALL FAMILY MEMBERS

In any communication process, there must be a listener and a speaker. For communication to be effective, the individuals involved must learn when they are to be the speaker and when they are to be the listener. Therefore, the first step is having individuals take turns practicing being the speaker and the listener. Each person should practice assuming each role three to four times across several days. While practicing, keep the following guidelines in mind.

## GUIDELINES FOR THE LISTENER

1.  Only make statements that paraphrase what you heard. Do not infer what you THINK the speaker meant or what s/he may have intended to say.

2.  Use steady (but not necessarily constant) eye contact so that you convey visually to the speaker that you hear what s/he is saying.

3.  Do not become involved in any other activity while listening to the speaker, no matter how insignificant you believe that activity is. Give your undivided attention to the speaker at all times.

4.  Do not defend or explain your position until the speaker states that s/he believes you have heard and understood what was being said.

5.  Don't interrupt: It's difficult to hear when you are talking yourself.

6.  Clarify what you hear: Sum up or make clear your understanding of what is being said at the end of a statement or phrase. This will aid you in getting the correct message. It is also important to admit if you don't understand something.

7.  Reflect on what you hear: This is different from clarification. Reflection involves showing your spouse that you are aware or understand what s/he feels. In essence, you hold up a mirror so your spouse can see what he or she is saying.

8.  Summarizing: Both speaker and listener should always attempt to summarize their conversation so that no loose ends are remaining and both have a clear understanding of what has been discussed. A summary also allows a couple to set a direction for constructive follow-up.

## GUIDELINES FOR THE SPEAKER

1.  Use "I" statements in describing your position/thoughts/feelings. Do not engage in accusing or blaming your listener.

2.  Speak briefly (2 to 3 minutes at a time) and ask for the listener to repeat back to you what s/he heard. This is referred to as reflective listening.

3.  If the listener is inaccurate with his/her reflections, repeat what you said. It is your responsibility to convey a clear message and to ensure that the message has been accurately received.

4.  Speak attentively: Just as one listens attentively, one should also speak in the same manner, maintaining appropriate and direct eye contact and looking for body signals (facial or posture) that indicate the other person is listening.

5.  Phrase meaningful questions: One way to keep a conversation short (and unproductive) is to ask a question that can be answered by either a "Yes" or a "No." Instead, try to ask questions that lead to more of a response from the other person that will help you understand him/her better.

6.  Don't overtalk: Speak to the point and avoid drawn-out statements that "overtell" a story or reaction. This will give the other person a chance to clarify and reflect on what he or she hears from you.

7.  Accept silence: Sometimes one of the best ways to make a point is to pause or use a period of silence after speaking. This allows both you and your listener to digest what is being said.

8.  Don't cross-examine: Avoid firing questions at the other person when attempting to learn something during a conversation. The use of tact and diplomacy expresses respect and may serve as a far better means of learning what you need to know.

It is often helpful to practice these roles in the therapy session first and then at home. At home, family members should also videotape or audiotape the conversations for later review with their therapist.

# EVERYTHING IS ALWAYS NEGATIVE
# IN OUR HOUSE

## GOALS OF THE EXERCISE

1. To improve and increase the rate of positive verbal interactions between family members.
2. To create a more positive view of family life.
3. To improve family cohesion and increase the sense of engagement within the family unit.

## ADDITIONAL HOMEWORK THAT MAY BE APPLICABLE
## TO COMMUNICATION PROBLEMS

- What Am I Thinking When I Am Feeling Depressed?          Page 115
- Why Can't You Understand My Side for Once?          Pages 164, 166

## ADDITIONAL PROBLEMS FOR WHICH THIS EXERCISE MAY BE USEFUL

- Jealousy/Insecurity

## SUGGESTIONS FOR PROCESSING THIS EXERCISE WITH THE CLIENT

Families experiencing difficulties with communication are often high in conflict and low in cohesiveness. Interactions tend to be more negative than positive. As a result, the number of interactions tends to decrease as members seek to avoid the conflicts that typically prevail. Thus in such a situation it is important for family members to increase the frequency of positive exchanges. This requires quite a bit of effort. At first, family members will feel that they are being insincere with one another. Explain that this is not unusual and should be expected at first. Let them know that sometimes changes in our beliefs and perceptions need to start with behavioral changes. The following exercise targets the behavior change needed to decrease the communication problems and conflicts.

# EVERYTHING IS ALWAYS NEGATIVE IN OUR HOUSE

## FOR ALL FAMILY MEMBERS

This exercise is designed for you and your family to find ways of focusing on, and increasing, the amount of positive interactions between you. Each family member should participate in this exercise. Each of you will need some index cards and a pen/pencil to write with.

1. Each family member is to identify five (5) characteristics that s/he likes about herself/himself. This list of positive characteristics should then be shared with all family members.

2. Have each family member also list at least five (5) things that s/he would like others to do for her/him and share this list as well.

3. For at least three (3) days over the next week, each family member is to select another person's list out of a hat. That day s/he is to do at least one thing or say at least one thing from the list of the family member that s/he has selected.

# REMEMBER WHEN . . .

## GOALS OF THE EXERCISE

1. To describe your thoughts and feelings about the person who passed away.
2. To experience a healthy way to grieve/mourn.
3. For family members to provide support to one another and mourn together.
4. To create a memory album that can serve as a keepsake.

## ADDITIONAL HOMEWORK THAT MAY BE APPLICABLE TO DEATH/LOSS

- What Am I Thinking When I Am Feeling Depressed?      Page 115
- Creating a Positive Outlook                          Page 227
- A Picture Is Worth a Thousand Words (just pictures 1–3)   Page 215

## ADDITIONAL PROBLEMS IN WHICH THIS EXERCISE MAY BE USEFUL

- Depression
- Adoption
- Foster Care

## SUGGESTIONS FOR PROCESSING THIS EXERCISE WITH THE CLIENT

The death of a loved one is always difficult. Many of us grieve in different ways and for different lengths of time. Sometimes this grief takes such a strong hold on us that it is difficult to move on with one's life. Sometimes individuals feel that if they give up the feelings of grief they will be giving up the memory of their loved one. One way let to go of the feelings of grief without "forgetting" about your loved one is by creating a memory album. A memory album can be comprised of pictures as well as words.

# REMEMBER WHEN . . .

To start, schedule a time for the family to get together. Have various materials available to make a memory album. These materials could include pictures, drawings, crayons or markers, glue, etc.

Decide whether you want to make one album or if each family member desires to make his or her own album to remember their loved one who has passed.

Make a title page for your memory album. You could color it or decorate it any way you wish.

As you peruse the pictures you've gathered over the years, try to recall stories you remember and discuss them with each other.

Inside the album describe your memories of _____ (the decedent). Start with your earliest memory of him or her. You might want to draw this or find a picture that describes your memory. Title the picture or drawing as well and indicate the date when the memory occurred.

Write, draw, or use a picture that describes one of your favorite memories of your loved one. _____

_____

_____

_____

_____

_____

_____

_____

Write, draw, or use a picture to describe the last thing you did with _____ (person who passed away). Write and/or draw the feeling you had.

_____

_____

_____

_____

Write, draw, or use a picture to describe three positive memories/images that you will never forget about _____.

# UNTIL WE MEET AGAIN, LOVE,

## GOALS OF THE EXERCISE

1. To describe and express your thoughts and feelings about the person who passed away.
2. To experience a healthy way to grieve/mourn.
3. For family members to provide support to one another and mourn together.

## ADDITIONAL HOMEWORK THAT MAY BE APPLICABLE TO DEATH/LOSS

- What Am I Thinking When I Am Feeling Depressed?          Page 115
- Creating a Positive Outlook          Page 227
- A Picture Is Worth a Thousand Words (just pictures 1–3)          Page 215

## ADDITIONAL PROBLEMS IN WHICH THIS EXERCISE MAY BE USEFUL

- Depression
- Adoption
- Foster Care

## SUGGESTIONS FOR PROCESSING THIS EXERCISE WITH THE CLIENT

When someone we love dies, we are filled with a range of emotions. Sometimes we feel so overwhelmed that it is difficult to express ourselves or even get in touch with our emotions. We know that writing is a great way to help us formulate our thoughts and feelings and helps us express our emotions. The following exercise can serve as a guide in helping individuals compose a letter to their loved one who have passed.

A session can involve the reading of the letters. This can also be done at the grave site as well.

# UNTIL WE MEET AGAIN,
# LOVE,

You can use the following questions and sentence stems to write a letter expressing your thoughts and feelings.

Describe the cause of death.

_____

_____

_____

_____

Write, draw, or use a picture to describe how you heard about the news of the death. Where were you at the time and who informed you?

_____

_____

_____

_____

_____

_____

_____

_____

Write, draw, or use a picture to describe what you do remember thinking and feeling at the time. _____

_____

_____

_____

_____

Write, draw, or use a picture to describe the service/funeral.

Describe a time(s) when it was just you and the person who passed.

Describe a time(s) when you and your family were with the person who passed.

Describe one of your favorite memories of your loved one.

_____

_____

_____

_____

Describe a time when you were worried about your loved one.

_____

_____

_____

_____

_____

Describe a time you were angry at your loved one.

_____

_____

_____

_____

_____

_____

_____

Describe what you admire most about the person who passed.

_____

_____

_____

_____

_____

_____

Write, draw, or use a picture to describe any unresolved feelings you have about _____ and how you would have wanted it to be resolved.

_____

_____

_____

_____

_____

_____

_____

_____

_____

_____

Compose a letter incorporating all or some of the prior information.

Decide if each of you wants to read your letters at the grave site, at your next session, or at home as part of a family meeting.

# THE QUESTIONS, FEELINGS, COMMENTS/CONCERNS GAME

## GOALS OF THE EXERCISE

1. To describe your thoughts and feelings about the person who has passed.
2. To create an openness to discussing the death or loss.
3. For family members to provide support to one another.
4. To reduce the isolation and awkwardness brought on by the death or loss.

## ADDITIONAL HOMEWORK THAT MAY BE APPLICABLE TO DEATH AND LOSS

- What Am I Thinking When I Am Feeling Depressed?       Page 115
- Creating a Positive Outlook       Page 227
- A Picture Is Worth a Thousand Words (just pictures 1–3)       Page 215

## ADDITIONAL PROBLEMS IN WHICH THIS EXERCISE MAY BE USEFUL

- Abuse
- Adoption
- Alcohol Abuse
- Depression
- Eating Disorders
- Reuniting Estranged Family Members

## SUGGESTIONS FOR PROCESSING THIS EXERCISE WITH THE CLIENT

Although death and loss are a part of life, they are frequently difficult experiences to endure. Families can become overwhelmed, shut down, isolated, or become overly involved in other activities as a means of avoiding talking about the pain associated with the death or loss. Since these subjects can often be difficult to address, the following game is an attempt to approach the subject in a less threatening manner. You can play the game in your office and then have the family continue it at home.

# THE QUESTIONS, FEELINGS, COMMENTS/CONCERNS GAME

You will need three different stacks of colored index cards, a pen or pencil for each family member, two (poker) chips for each family member, and a single die from a set of dice.

Each family member is to generate at least five responses to each of the following three categories.

Responses should be on color-coded index cards. Each color will represent a separate category.

1.  QUESTIONS I HAVE ABOUT THE DEATH OR LOSS.

2.  FEELINGS I HAVE OR I THINK SOMEONE ELSE HAS ABOUT THE DEATH OR LOSS.

3.  **COMMENTS OR CONCERNS** I HAVE ABOUT THE DEATH OR LOSS.

As family members sort all the cards into the three respective piles, each person rolls a single die.

If a person rolls a 1 or 2, s/he picks and responds to a card from the QUESTIONS pile.

If a person rolls a 3 or 4, s/he picks and responds to a card from the FEELINGS pile.

If a person rolls a 5 or 6, s/he picks and responds to a card from the COMMENTS/ CONCERNS pile.

Each member has two PASSES. A PASS can be used any time a person wants to give his/her card or turn to someone else. The member using a PASS will have to give one of their chips to the person they choose to take their turn.

After responding to a card, other family members are encouraged to answer as well. When no other responses are being offered, the next member takes a turn.

# DEPENDENCY GO AWAY

## GOALS OF THE EXERCISE

1. To identify dependent thinking patterns.
2. To generate alternative thinking patterns to help challenge dependent behaviors.
3. To gain support from family members to change dependent thinking styles and behaviors.

## ADDITIONAL HOMEWORK THAT MAY BE APPLICABLE TO DEPENDENCY ISSUES

- What Am I Thinking When I Am Feeling Depressed?      Page 115
- When I Feel Anxious It Is Like . . .      Page 42
- Acting as If      Page 52

## ADDITIONAL PROBLEMS IN WHICH THIS EXERCISE MAY BE USEFUL

- Anxiety
- Depression

## SUGGESTIONS FOR PROCESSING THIS EXERCISE WITH FAMILY MEMBERS

Individuals struggling with dependency are often anxious and fearful of many things such as abandonment. This fear reinforces their behavior. It is difficult for them to challenge their fears. This exercise is designed to help dependent individuals learn to challenge their fears and identify alternative ways of thinking and perceiving.

# DEPENDENCY GO AWAY

Over the next week, each family member should take time to notice and identify situations in which dependent behaviors are exhibited. Describe the dependent behaviors below.

_____

_____

_____

_____

_____

_____

For each behavior and situation, family members should try to identify thoughts to explain the behavior as a way of developing understanding of the fear (e.g., abandonment or being alone) underlying the thinking.

_____

_____

_____

_____

_____

_____

As a way to challenge the fearful thoughts, brainstorm beliefs one would have in order to not be fearful. This should be done as a family. One could also ask other family members or friends to share their beliefs about the fear in order to contrast these beliefs with those of the dependent family member.

_____

_____

_____

_____

_____

_____

_____

Describe the pros and cons of adopting competing thoughts and perceptions with being fearful.

| PROS | CONS |
|---|---|
| _____ | _____ |
| _____ | _____ |
| _____ | _____ |
| _____ | _____ |
| _____ | _____ |
| _____ | _____ |
| _____ | _____ |
| _____ | _____ |
| _____ | _____ |
| _____ | _____ |

For each family member, try to describe how life would be different if the dependency behaviors were significantly reduced.

_____

_____

_____

_____

_____

_____

_____

This homework can also be divided into sections and assigned over a few weeks.

# DO I HAVE TO BE DEPRESSED?

## GOALS OF THE EXERCISE

1. Identify times and situations when family members tend to be feeling depressed.
2. Increase family members' ability to self-monitor.
3. Learn to challenge the belief of powerlessness
4. Increase a sense of choice to change depressive thoughts and behaviors.

## ADDITIONAL HOMEWORK THAT MAY BE APPLICABLE TO DEPRESSION

- My Safe Place                                                   Page 19
- When I Feel Anxious It Is Like . . .                            Page 42
- Creating a Positive Outlook                                     Page 227
- A Picture Is Worth a Thousand Words (just pictures 1–3)         Page 215

## ADDITIONAL PROBLEMS IN WHICH THIS EXERCISE MAY BE USEFUL

- Addictions
- Anxiety
- Anger

## SUGGESTIONS FOR PROCESSING THIS EXERCISE WITH FAMILY MEMBERS

This exercise is to help family members to identify and describe their experience with depression. It is designed to help individuals connect thoughts with feelings and behaviors. The more a person is aware of his/her thoughts and behaviors with regard to his/her feelings, the more empowered that person can become to make changes. The exercise is also developed to help individuals realize that they can choose to think and/or behave differently even when feeling depressed.

# DO I HAVE TO BE DEPRESSED?

This exercise will help you express how you think and behave when experiencing depression. The more you are aware of your self-talk and actions when feeling depressed, the better equipped you may become to make changes. Take some time during the next week to think about times you are feeling down or depressed. Complete the statements below during such times to help you increase your awareness of your thoughts and behaviors during such times. Once you have done so, you can begin to challenge yourself to try and think and behave differently.

## FOR THE FAMILY MEMBER WHO IS DEPRESSED

List what you think when you feel depressed. This should be shared with all family members.

When I think _____ I feel depressed.

When I think _____ I feel depressed.

When I think _____ I feel depressed.

When I think _____ I feel depressed.

When I think _____ I feel depressed.

List what you do when you feel depressed. This should be shared with all family members.

When I do _____ I feel depressed.

When I do _____ I feel depressed.

When I do _____ I feel depressed.

When I do _____ I feel depressed.

When I do _____ I feel depressed.

I am not depressed when I think about _____

_____

I am not depressed when I think about _____

_____

I am not depressed when I think about _____

_____

I am not depressed when I am doing _____

_____

I am not depressed when I am doing _____

_____

I am not depressed when I am doing _____

_____

When I am feeling down or depressed I will read the above statements explaining **thoughts I can have** and **activities I can do**. I know that such thoughts and behaviors are healthier for me and will help me feel less down or depressed.
I want to feel less depressed for the following reasons:

_____

_____

_____

_____

_____


_____

Your Signature

# MY POSITIVE SCRIPT

## GOALS OF THE EXERCISE

1. Increase sense of awareness of self-talk.
2. Learn to replace negative dialogues with positive.
3. Increase sense of choice to change depressive thoughts.

## ADDITIONAL HOMEWORK THAT MAY BE APPLICABLE TO DEPRESSION

- My Safe Place                                            Page 19
- When I Feel Anxious It Is Like . . .                     Page 42
- Creating a Positive Outlook                              Page 227
- A Picture Is Worth a Thousand Words (just pictures 1–3)  Page 215

## ADDITIONAL PROBLEMS IN WHICH THIS EXERCISE MAY BE USEFUL

- Addictions
- Anxiety
- Anger

## SUGGESTIONS FOR PROCESSING THIS EXERCISE WITH FAMILY MEMBER(S)

Individuals struggling with depression are often stuck thinking in negative ways about themselves, their situation, and/or their future. This negative talk is often repetitive. They can repeat it as if it was a script from a movie. The idea of this exercise is to help them create a new script to recite.

# MY POSITIVE SCRIPT

If you are like most people who struggle with depression, then you probably also spend a fair amount of time beating yourself up. These negative comments can seem so repetitive that they can be like memorized lines from a movie script. Sometimes these negative scripts can be very automatic and intrusive. You may want to think in a more positive way, which is usually easier said than done. This exercise is designed to make that task a little easier. When we are feeling depressed and thinking negatively it is difficult to come up with alternative and more adaptive positive thoughts. One way to do this is to plan for such situations. By writing the "Positive Script" out ahead of time, you will not have to work so hard. You will just need to read what you write here.

Over the next week try to notice times you are engaging in a negative script.

An example of a negative script might involve the following.

"I'm such a dumb *^#^**. I can't do anything right the first time. What a loser." No wonder people don't like me, I don't even like myself."

When you notice that you are in that spot again and thinking negatively, write down what you are thinking about and telling yourself, BUT skip lines like the example above. _____

_____

_____

_____

_____

_____

Now go back and cross out the negative comments and, on the lines above, write down what you would rather say. If it helps, think of what you would want someone you care about to say.

I made a mistake. I guess I'm human like everyone else.

~~"I'm such a dumb *^#^**. I can't do anything right the first time. What a loser.~~

Now write it one more time without including the negative script.

I made a mistake. I guess I'm human like everyone else.

_____

_____

_____

Keep the positive scripts and keep adding to it whenever you can. You deserve it!

# SOMEONE IN MY FAMILY IS DEPRESSED

## GOALS OF THE EXERCISE

1. Determine the family member's understanding about depression.
2. Identify how other family members feel affected by the family member with depression.
3. Identify triggers to the depression.
4. Develop ways to demonstrate affective support to the family member with depression.

## ADDITIONAL HOMEWORK THAT MAY BE APPLICABLE TO DEPRESSION

- My Safe Place                                                    Page 19
- When I Feel Anxious It Is Like . . .                             Page 42
- Creating a Positive Outlook                                      Page 227
- A Picture Is Worth a Thousand Words (just pictures 1–3)          Page 215

## ADDITIONAL PROBLEMS IN WHICH THIS EXERCISE MAY BE USEFUL

- Anger
- Anxiety
- Behavioral Problems

## SUGGESTIONS FOR PROCESSING THIS EXERCISE WITH THE CLIENT

This exercise is designed for all family members to complete and then to discuss, either in a family meeting or in a family session.

# SOMEONE IN MY FAMILY IS DEPRESSED

## FOR EACH FAMILY MEMBER

This exercise is designed for all family members to complete and then discuss, either in a family meeting or in a family session.

Define "depression": _____

_____

What does _____ do that tells me he/she is depressed? Try to identify at least four situations.

1.  He/she _____

    _____

    When he/she does this, I think and feel _____

    _____

2.  He/she _____

    _____

    When he/she does this, I think and feel _____

    _____

3.  He/she _____

    _____

    When he/she does this, I think and feel _____

    _____

4.  He/she _____

    _____

    When he/she does this, I think and feel _____

    _____

# WHAT AM I THINKING WHEN I AM FEELING DEPRESSED?

## GOALS OF THE EXERCISE

1. Identify the various thoughts that go through an individual's mind when feeling depressed.
2. Identify possible triggers to the depression.

## ADDITIONAL HOMEWORK THAT MAY BE APPLICABLE TO DEPRESSION

- My Safe Place       Page 19
- When I Feel Anxious It Is Like . . .       Page 42
- Creating a Positive Outlook       Page 227
- A Picture Is Worth a Thousand Words (just pictures 1–3)       Page 215

## ADDITIONAL PROBLEMS FOR WHICH THIS EXERCISE MAY BE USEFUL

- Addictions
- Anger
- Anxiety
- Communication Problems
- Eating Disorders

## SUGGESTIONS FOR PROCESSING THIS EXERCISE WITH CLIENT

Have all family members choose the cognitive distortions they tend to engage in, and have them give an example of each one. (See the exercise "My/Our Daughter Is Depressed" (pages 119–120) for a list of common cognitive distortions.)

# WHAT AM I THINKING WHEN I AM FEELING DEPRESSED?

## FOR ALL FAMILY MEMBERS

At times, our thoughts can greatly influence how we feel. One of the first steps to changing how we feel is to identify how we think. By completing this exercise, you will learn how you sometimes think and perceive things.

This week I _____

_____

This was an example of the following cognitive distortion _____

This week I _____

_____

This was an example of the following cognitive distortion _____

This week I _____

_____

This was an example of the following cognitive distortion _____

# WHAT DO OTHERS VALUE ABOUT ME?

## GOALS OF THE EXERCISE

1. To develop a sense of value.
2. To develop a stronger sense of self-worth.

## ADDITIONAL HOMEWORK THAT MAY BE APPLICABLE TO DEPRESSION

## ADDITIONAL PROBLEMS IN WHICH THIS EXERCISE MAY BE USEFUL

- Anger
- Anxiety

## SUGGESTIONS FOR PROCESSING THIS EXERCISE WITH THE CLIENT

Many individuals who suffer from depression report feeling a lack of value. To counter such negative thinking, have them complete the exercise on the following page.

# WHAT DO OTHERS VALUE ABOUT ME?

This exercise is designed to help you challenge your belief or view of how valued you are by others.

Seek out at least two family members and two friends, and ask them, "What do you value about me?" Record their responses verbatim.

1. _____ said that she/he values me because _____

   _____

2. _____ said that she/he values me because _____

   _____

3. _____ said that she/he values me because _____

   _____

4. _____ said that she/he values me because _____

   _____

Share the findings with some other family members, then have those family members record times when they observe the evidence of this value (e.g., you are thoughtful, you helped Johnny with his homework).

# MY/OUR DAUGHTER IS DEPRESSED

## GOALS OF THE EXERCISE

1. Help the depressed child/adolescent identify various thinking errors (distorted thoughts) that lead to depression.
2. Begin to generate a sense of control over feeling depressed.

## ADDITIONAL HOMEWORK THAT MAY BE APPLICABLE TO DEPRESSION

- My Safe Place                                                    Page 19
- When I Feel Anxious It Is Like . . .                             Page 42
- Creating a Positive Outlook                                      Page 227
- A Picture Is Worth a Thousand Words (just pictures 1–3)          Page 215

## ADDITIONAL PROBLEMS IN WHICH THIS EXERCISE MAY BE USEFUL

- Addictions
- Anger
- Anxiety
- Communication Problems

## SUGGESTIONS FOR PROCESSING THIS EXERCISE WITH THE CLIENT

This exercise is a fun way for family members to become familiar with the various types of cognitive distortions that individuals sometimes engage in. At times, our thoughts can influence how we feel and perceive situations. This exercise is designed to help family members become more aware of cognitive distortions and to begin to aid them in identifying which distortions they tend to engage in.

# MY/OUR DAUGHTER IS DEPRESSED

## FOR ALL FAMILY MEMBERS

This exercise is a fun way for family members to become familiar with the various types of cognitive distortions that individuals sometimes engage in. At times, our thoughts can influence how we feel and perceive situations. This exercise is designed to help you become more aware of cognitive distortions and to identify ones you may engage in.

After reading the definition and accompanying example for each of the following thinking errors that many people make, see if you can find them in the word search on page 120.

- **Catastrophizing.** This is when you think about consequences and you blow them out of proportion in a negative way. For example, after striking out at bat, Joe says to himself, "I'll never get a hit. The coach will probably cut me from the team now. I'll never be able to play baseball again."

- **Overgeneralization**. This is when you think of one example to make conclusions about a number of other things, or all similar circumstances. For example, Tim breaks up with his girlfriend Becky, and Becky thinks to herself, "Guys are scum, and Tim is just like all the rest of them."

- **Fortune telling**. This is when you predict that negative things will happen to you in the future, based on little or no supporting evidence. For example, T.J. wants to play basketball for his school but begins to think, "They won't want me to play, I won't be as good as the other kids."

- **Black-and-white thinking**. This is when you look at situations, others, or even yourself as being totally bad or totally good—without any sense of balance. For example, Susan is thinking about her parents getting on her case about her schoolwork, and she concludes, "I can never come home without having them get on my case. Every day it's the same thing."

- **Dark glasses or mental filtering**. This is when you block out all the positives and just focus on the negatives. For example, Mike brings home all As and Bs on his report card except for one D. He thinks to himself repeatedly, "I am so dumb I can't even get better than a D."

- **Personalizing**. This is when you take on the responsibility for something that is not your job. For example, Sondra arranges to have pizza delivered to her house for a party she is having. The delivery person gets lost and never arrives with the pizza. She thinks to herself, "I should have never called that place. Why couldn't I have called the other pizza store?"

- **Discounting**. This is when you reject the positive things that happen to you. For example, Michelle's girlfriend tells Michelle that her outfit looks great, but Michelle thinks to herself, "This outfit looks terrible on me. She is just trying to say something nice but doesn't really mean it."

- **Judging**. This is when you are critical of yourself or others and make statements such as, "I should be more relaxed," "I ought to know by now," "I have to get this right."

- **Mind reading**. This is when you make a negative assumption regarding other people's thoughts and behaviors. For example, Bryan passes a girl in the hall and when she does not say hello to him, he thinks, "She hates me. I don't stand a chance with her."

| C | A | T | A | S | T | R | O | P | H | I | Z | I | N | G | B |
| M | D | F | O | S | R | F | G | H | J | K | B | L | F | B | L |
| I | A | F | V | J | K | L | W | Z | Y | B | J | S | O | J | A |
| N | W | G | R | Y | T | I | T | A | P | Q | G | H | R | K | C |
| D | O | F | R | Q | S | C | G | H | J | K | N | M | T | T | K |
| J | U | D | G | I | N | G | U | H | Q | S | D | D | U | R | W |
| P | M | U | E | E | A | F | J | I | V | S | F | A | N | A | H |
| A | G | G | N | I | Z | I | L | A | N | O | S | R | E | P | I |
| D | G | W | A | K | R | K | O | D | W | V | K | K | T | O | T |
| Q | K | O | R | U | G | Y | N | F | D | E | B | G | L | W | E |
| L | K | U | L | V | S | J | W | N | C | U | O | L | L | N | T |
| Q | W | G | I | L | T | E | R | I | N | G | K | A | L | W | H |
| K | U | H | Z | G | N | I | T | N | U | O | C | S | I | D | I |
| L | C | Z | I | B | T | D | J | N | K | S | V | S | N | N | N |
| K | M | I | N | D | R | E | A | D | I | N | G | E | G | P | K |
| S | Q | G | G | H | E | A | X | C | K | T | D | S | M | L | I |
| S | E | L | F | B | L | A | M | I | N | G | D | F | N | J | N |
| Q | F | S | O | L | B | N | G | K | J | X | G | E | J | K | G |

# CIRCLES OF PERCEPTION

## GOALS OF THE EXERCISE

1. To solicit family members' perception of their relationships to one another, particularly in those who have difficulty with verbal expression.
2. To implement an activity that will facilitate individual work, followed by an in-session collaboration.
3. To exchange ideas and perceptions of each other and broaden family members' conceptualizations of how they view themselves.

## ADDITIONAL HOMEWORK THAT MAY BE APPLICABLE TO DISILLUSIONMENT WITH FAMILY TIES

- What Am I Thinking When I Am Feeling Depressed?         Page 115

## ADDITIONAL PROBLEMS IN WHICH THIS EXERCISE MAY BE USEFUL

- Anger Problems
- Communication Problems
- Dependency
- Disengagement
- Jealousy/Insecurity

## SUGGESTIONS FOR PROCESSING THIS EXERCISE WITH CLIENT

Weekes and Treat (1992) first introduced the use of circles as a strategy in their work with couples. It was later expounded on by Dattilio (2000), who also applied it to couples and later to his work with families (Dattilio, 1997; 2001). This technique can be used in-session; however, with families it may be more effective as a task assignment, particularly with younger children who may want to elaborate on their schematic diagrams with crayons or colored pens.

# CIRCLES OF PERCEPTION

Trying to express in words how we see things can often be difficult. This is especially true when it pertains to families and family members.

Sometimes, a simpler way to do this is to express what we see and how we feel through creative visual designs. Sometimes, the simpler the drawing, the better we are able to get our point across to others. This exercise is designed to help you express your perception of your family as you view it currently and how you would like it to be in the future. Try to be as honest as you can when constructing both drawings. Try not to worry too much about how the other family members may view your designs.

1.  Take a clean piece of white paper (unlined). You can use a regular graphite pencil, colored pencils, or even crayons or colored ink pens. Using only one circle to represent each family member, draw how you view your family constellation as it exists. The closer the circles are, the more they indicate how emotionally close you feel those family members are to one another. So, for example, your drawing may look similar to any of the following designs.

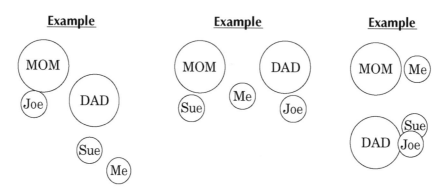

The large circles represent the parents or grandparents (adults) and the smaller circles represent the children.

After you have completed your drawing, take the other plain piece of paper, marking it Number 2. Using the same type of circles, draw how you would like to see your family ideally.

Bring both of your drawings to the next session and be prepared to discuss the following:

1.  Explain your drawings.

2.  How did you feel about doing this exercise?

3.  Did it make you think more about how your family members relate to one another?

4.  Did you find the task difficult to do?

5.  Did you notice a big difference between your first drawing and the second drawing?

6.  In what ways did your drawings differ from those of other family members?

# I NEED TO GET CONTROL

## GOALS OF THE EXERCISE

1.  To gain some control over the frequency of eating/dieting/weight-controlling behaviors.
2.  To get a sense of how often these behaviors are occurring.

## ADDITIONAL HOMEWORK THAT MAY BE APPLICABLE TO EATING DISORDERS

## ADDITIONAL PROBLEMS IN WHICH THIS EXERCISE MAY BE USEFUL

*   Addictions
*   Anger

## SUGGESTIONS FOR PROCESSING THIS EXERCISE WITH THE CLIENT

Many children and adolescents, especially females, are at risk of developing some type of eating disorder. The heavy emphasis in our society to be thin reinforces the idea of having a slender and well-defined body. This need to fit into society's expectations can quickly spin out of control and become an obsession. Some of the most effective treatment interventions have relied on the use of linking one's thoughts and behaviors. As a result, the following exercise utilizes a cognitive-behavioral approach.

# I NEED TO GET CONTROL

## FOR THE FAMILY MEMBER EXPERIENCING AN EATING DISORDER

1. On the charts provided record the times that you engage in any kind of eating/dieting/weight control behavior (e.g., not eating a meal, purging).
2. Describe how you are feeling before, during, and after this behavior.
3. Describe what you are thinking before, during, and after this behavior.
4. Share this with the other family members at your next family therapy session.

| Behavior | | Thought | Feeling | Day | Time |
|---|---|---|---|---|---|
| | Before | | | | |
| | During | | | | |
| | After | | | | |

| Behavior | | Thought | Feeling | Day | Time |
|---|---|---|---|---|---|
| | Before | | | | |
| | During | | | | |
| | After | | | | |

| Behavior | | Thought | Feeling | Day | Time |
|---|---|---|---|---|---|
| | Before | | | | |
| | During | | | | |
| | After | | | | |

| Behavior | | Thought | Feeling | Day | Time |
|---|---|---|---|---|---|
| | Before | | | | |
| | During | | | | |
| | After | | | | |

# WHAT AM I THINKING?

## GOALS OF THE EXERCISE

1. To identify the types of thinking errors the individual engages in.
2. To identify the feeling you have when you think such thoughts.
3. To generate more adaptive/realistic self-talk and identify alternative responses.
4. Describe the feeling you have when you think about the alternative statement.

## ADDITIONAL HOMEWORK THAT MAY BE APPLICABLE TO EATING DISORDERS

- Staying Clean — Page 8
- What Else Can I Do? — Page 11
- My Safe Place — Page 19
- A Picture Is Worth a Thousand Words (just pictures 1–3) — Page 215
- What Am I Thinking When I Am Feeling Depressed? — Page 115
- What Do Others Value about Me? — Page 117
- Creating a Positive Outlook — Page 227

## ADDITIONAL PROBLEMS FOR WHICH THIS EXERCISE MAY BE USEFUL

- Addictions
- Anger
- Anxiety
- Depression

## SUGGESTIONS FOR PROCESSING THIS EXERCISE WITH THE CLIENT

Individuals with an eating disorder are constantly in their heads and engage in various types of cognitive distortions. They may think that if they start eating they won't be able to stop. They may believe that the only way to "look good" is to exercise and not eat. Such thoughts are generally based in some kind of fear (e.g., of becoming overweight, losing control, being rejected). It is important for these individuals to get such thoughts and fears out of their head and to externalize them.

# WHAT AM I THINKING?

## FOR THE PERSON EXPERIENCING AN EATING DISORDER

This exercise is designed to help you begin the process of getting control over your behaviors, thoughts, and feelings about eating, body weight, or body shape. Use the list of cognitive distortions from your personal experience that you discussed with your therapist to complete the following charts.

Dichotomous Thinking—Experiences are codified as either all or nothing (e.g., "I am either fat or not, there's no in-between").

Tunnel Vision—Seeing what fits one's current state of mind (e.g., "If I eat only foods with starch, I'll get fat and won't be able to lose the weight").

Mind Reading—Assuming what others are thinking without the benefit of verbal communication (e.g., "I know that when people look at me, they think that I am too fat").

Arbitrary Inference—Conclusions are made in the absence of substantiating evidence (e.g., "If I am not a perfect body weight, no one will like me").

Catastrophizing—This is when you think about consequences and you blow them out of proportion in a negative way. For example, you are counting points for a Weight Watchers program or calories for the day and you exceed your allotted number. You respond by thinking, "I can't believe I did that. I might as well give up now because I can never stick to anything."

Dark Glasses or Mental Filtering—This is when you block out the positives and just focus on the negatives. For example, two of your friends meet you at the mall. One friend remarks about how good you look. You begin to think that your other friend must believe you look pretty awful.

Discounting—This is when you reject the positive things that happen to you. For example, over a week's time, you refrain from purging for four days. Instead of looking at the positive, you think, "I am so weak, I purged on three days this past week."

| Behavior | Thought | Type of Distortion | Feeling |
|---|---|---|---|
| | | | |
| | | | |
| | | | |
| | | | |
| | | | |

| Alternative Thought | Feeling |
|---|---|
| | |
| | |
| | |
| | |
| | |

For each of the distortions, describe the reasons you could believe such thoughts to be true. _____

_____

_____

_____

_____

For each of the distortions, describe the reasons you could believe such thoughts could be false. _____

_____

_____

_____

_____

_____

# WHY IS SHE DOING THIS?

## GOALS OF THE EXERCISE

1. To allow each family member a chance to express his/her feelings regarding living with a family member with an eating disorder.
2. To help the therapist understand each family member's conceptualization of eating disorders.

## ADDITIONAL HOMEWORK THAT MAY BE APPLICABLE TO EATING DISORDERS

- Staying Clean                                               Page 8
- What Else Can I Do?                                         Page 11
- My Safe Place                                               Page 19
- A Picture Is Worth a Thousand Words (just pictures 1–3)     Page 215
- What Am I Thinking When I Am Feeling Depressed?             Page 115
- What Do Others Value about Me?                              Page 117
- Creating a Positive Outlook                                 Page 227

## ADDITIONAL PROBLEMS IN WHICH THIS EXERCISE MAY BE USEFUL

- Addictions
- Anger
- Anxiety
- Depression

## SUGGESTIONS FOR PROCESSING THIS EXERCISE WITH THE CLIENT

Family members may not have an accurate understanding of what the "problem" is regarding a family member who has an eating disorder. Learning what each family member perceives to be the problem and his/her feelings regarding this are important for the therapist to know in order to develop treatment plans.

# WHY IS SHE DOING THIS?

## FOR INDIVIDUALS WHO HAVE A FAMILY MEMBER WITH AN EATING DISORDER

The following exercise will help you construct your perception and understanding of an eating disorder. It will also help you identify how you feel about the situation and how to deal with the family member who has this problem.

1. Describe what an eating disorder is from your perspective.

   _____

   _____

   _____

   _____

2. What do you see or hear that makes you believe _____ has an eating disorder? _____

   _____

   _____

   _____

3. When you see _____ engaging in eating-disorder-like behaviors, how does that make you feel?

   _____

   _____

   _____

4. What do you wish you could do?

   _____

   _____

   _____

   _____

5.  How does _____ respond to you when you try to help?

    _____

    _____

    _____

    _____

6.  How does that make you feel?

    _____

    _____

7.  How could you be a support to _____?

    _____

    _____

    _____

# WE'RE NO LONGER SPEAKING TO ONE ANOTHER

## GOALS OF THE EXERCISE

1. Estranged family members will be able to make contact with one another in a civil fashion.
2. A resolution of differences will occur in an attempt to facilitate reunification.

## ADDITIONAL HOMEWORK THAT MAY BE APPLICABLE TO ESTRANGED FAMILY MEMBERS

- How Can I Talk So He'll Listen?                           Page 89
- Circles of Perception                                      Page 122
- Why Can't You Understand My Side of the Story for Once?    Pages 164, 166

## ADDITIONAL PROBLEMS FOR WHICH THIS MAY BE USEFUL

- Anger Management
- Communication Problems
- Disengagement/Loss of Family Cohesion
- Inheritance Disputes
- Jealousy/Insecurity
- Sexual Abuse

## SUGGESTIONS FOR PROCESSING THIS EXERCISE WITH CLIENT(S)

Family estrangements often occur for all types of reasons and can be very distressing to deal with. Oftentimes, family members may be cut off from one another for years, sometimes decades, causing much pain and suffering for all parties involved. Ultimately, a family member(s) needs to take action to make contact with estranged members and determine if the potential exists for unification. This is the first step in the reunification process.

# WE'RE NO LONGER SPEAKING TO ONE ANOTHER

## GETTING IN TOUCH WITH YOUR THOUGHTS AND FEELINGS

1.  How has the family estrangement affected me?

    _____

    _____

    _____

2.  What are my thoughts and beliefs about it?

    Thoughts: _____

    _____

    Beliefs: _____

    _____

    Where do these thoughts and beliefs come from and how did they form?

    _____

    _____

    _____

3.  What are my emotions about the entire conflict and subsequent estrangement?

    _____

    _____

    _____

4.  How has the above changed my behaviors?

    _____

    _____

    _____

# I MISS YOU

## GOALS OF THE EXERCISE

1. To find an acceptable balance between tension and not speaking to one another (emotional cutoffs).
2. Reduce to eliminate the conflict that led to the estrangement.
3. To reduce the need for power/control and punishing one another through emotional cutoffs.
4. To facilitate ultimate reunification.

## ADDITIONAL HOMEWORK THAT MAY BE APPLICABLE TO ESTRANGEMENT

- My Safe Place                                     Page 19
- What Happens When I Become Angry                  Page 28
- Creating a Positive Outlook                       Page 227

## ADDITIONAL PROBLEMS FOR WHICH THIS MAY BE USEFUL

- Poor Communication
- Disengagement
- Jealousy
- Anger

## SUGGESTIONS FOR PROCESSING THIS EXERCISE WITH FAMILY MEMBERS

Many family members fined dealing with the estrangement extremely difficult and uncomfortable. One way to help them through the process is to recommend assigned readings such as Datillio and Nichols (2010) and Christensen and Jacobsen (2000).

# I MISS YOU

The following activity is designed to help family members accept the need for intervention strategies to set in and allow time for the healing to occur:

1.  What do I need to do to give comfort to myself during the process of reunification?

    Cognitively: _____

    _____

    Emotionally: _____

    _____

    Behaviorally: _____

    _____

2.  How will I go on if the reunification process fails?

    _____

    _____

3.  How can I best strengthen my family ties?

    _____

    _____

For the family member contemplating making contact with the estranged family members:

1.  Think about how you want to approach the estranged family member(s). What would you like to say to them? Should you e-mail them, send them a handwritten letter, or call them on the phone?

    _____

    _____

2.  What happens if I'm rejected?

    Alternatives:

    a.  I could contact them through a different medium.

    b.  I could use an intermediary such as a friend, relative, or even a mental health professional.

3. If this fails, can I wait a while longer and make a later attempt at the same task?

_____

_____

List the:

**PROS**                                    **CONS**

_____     _____

_____     _____

_____     _____

_____     _____

_____     _____

4. If contact is made, what are my fears?  What am I willing to offer as a means of concession in order to facilitate reunification?

_____

_____

   a. Admitting that I was wrong.
      List how: _____

   b. What am I willing to concede to?

   _____

   _____

   c. What responsibility should I accept for my role in the estrangement?

   _____

   _____

   d. What do I want from the other family member(s)?

   _____

   _____

5. How can I process my resentment when I see my family member(s)?
   a. Write out my thoughts and feelings.
   b. Role play how I will express my resentments to others.

6.  What are my fantasies about what life will be like after the reunification is made?

    _____

    _____

7.  What type of steps can I take to prevent future misunderstandings or estrangements?

    a.  Methods for processing anger that may develop:

    _____

    _____

    b.  Methods for processing old resentments:

    _____

    _____

# A CHANGING OF THE GUARD

## GOALS OF THE EXERCISE

1. Achieve some boundaries regarding who is in charge of a family business.
2. Resolve issues of ownership and power in a family business.
3. Formalize the transition of a new generation carrying on the family business.

## ADDITIONAL HOMEWORK THAT MAY BE APPLICABLE TO FAMILY BUSINESS CONFLICTS

- Why Can't You Understand My Side for Once?          Pages 164, 166

## ADDITIONAL PROBLEMS FOR WHICH THIS EXERCISE MAY BE USEFUL

- Blended Families
- Disengagement*

## SUGGESTIONS FOR PROCESSING THIS EXERCISE WITH THE CLIENT

A family business has many positives, but there can also be some awkward and uncomfortable times. This is especially true when the next generation is given the reins and expected to run the business. Sometimes those who have been in charge have difficulty giving up their control, and still want the final say. It is important for family members to discuss and come to terms regarding who maintains what role and what that role means. As a way to signify the changing of the guard, so to speak, it is oftentimes beneficial to have a ceremony.

---

*This problem is not specifically discussed in detail in this volume.

# A CHANGING OF THE GUARD

The following exercise is designed to help those family members who are currently in charge to hand over the reins to the new leaders or bosses.

1. Have those family members who are currently in charge purchase or design a big key, to symbolize the keys to the business.

2. Suggest that the family go out to dinner together and recommend that the current members in charge make a speech announcing the names of the family members who will from this time forward (or starting on a specific date) be the new bosses.

3. At the end of the speech present the key to the new bosses.

# WHO IS DOING WHAT?

## GOALS OF THE EXERCISE

1. Establish guidelines for boundaries and define roles of each family member in a family business.
2. Achieve agreement regarding the levels of power and responsibilities among family members in a family business.

## ADDITIONAL HOMEWORK THAT MAY BE APPLICABLE TO FAMILY BUSINESS CONFLICTS

- Why Can't You Understand My Side for Once?        Pages 164, 166

## ADDITIONAL PROBLEMS FOR WHICH THIS EXERCISE MAY BE USEFUL

- Blended Families
- Family Conflicts around House Chores[*]

## SUGGESTIONS FOR PROCESSING THIS EXERCISE WITH THE CLIENT

Once a changing of the guard in a family business is official, family members still need to identify who is responsible for what aspects of the business. One area of conflict that frequently arises during such transitions involves how things have been conducted in the past and the way in which the next generation wants things to work. Another salient issue has to do with the amount of say and control those who have turned over the keys still maintain.

---

[*]This problem is not specifically discussed in detail in this volume.

# WHO IS DOING WHAT?

## FOR FAMILY MEMBERS INVOLVED IN A FAMILY BUSINESS

The following exercise will help you to establish guidelines for boundaries and define roles of each member in the family business. Each person involved should read and respond to the first two items by him/herself.

1. Have family members identify their skills and strengths. (This can be used for a family discussion in the next session.)

2. Have family members put in writing the needs of the business. It would be helpful to have those who were most recently in charge, as well as those who have just transitioned into that role, to identify the goals/objectives of the business for the coming year.

3. Have the family meet as a group and match the skills/strengths of each family member to the various roles and responsibilities within the business.

# THANKS, BUT NO THANKS

## GOALS OF THE EXERCISE

1. Reduce the marital and family conflict regarding family-of-origin interference with family issues.
2. Identify the thoughts and feelings associated with the interferences.

## ADDITIONAL HOMEWORK THAT MAY BE APPLICABLE TO FAMILY-OF-ORIGIN INTERFERENCE

- Acting as If                                          Page 52
- How Can I Talk So He'll Listen?                       Page 89
- Why Can't You Understand My Side for Once?            Pages 164, 166
- I Am Not Jealous                                      Page 171

## ADDITIONAL PROBLEMS FOR WHICH THIS EXERCISE MAY BE USEFUL

- Communication Problems
- Jealousy/Insecurity

## SUGGESTIONS FOR PROCESSING THIS EXERCISE WITH THE CLIENT

The well-meaning intentions of parents, grandparents, and other family-of-origin members can at times become very destructive forces—especially when such input is unwelcome or uninvited. The marital dyad will frequently argue over their spouse's family-of-origin stepping over the boundary lines. Children/adolescents will also begin to act out emotionally and behaviorally as the result of such interference. Therefore, the couple and their children/adolescents need to find a way to establish boundaries. Another key is developing a sense of cohesion as a family unit.

# THANKS, BUT NO THANKS

## FOR THE COUPLE EXPERIENCING FAMILY-OF-ORIGIN INTERFERENCE WITH FAMILY ISSUES

The following exercise is designed to help you gain a clearer perspective of your concerns as a couple regarding the involvement of other family members in your family issues. You will need paper and pen to record some lists. Find some quiet time in which the two of you can complete the following exercise:

1. As a couple, identify your perceptions of the interactions with other family members. You can do this individually first and then compare your lists.

2. Once the perceptions are identified, designate the accompanying feelings by using "I" statements.

3. As a couple, practice effective communication skills and active listening. (See the homework on Communication Problems, pages 89, 90, 92.)

# HOW CAN I TELL HER TO MIND HER OWN BUSINESS?

## GOALS OF THE EXERCISE

1. Establish boundaries and limits regarding the roles of family-of-origin family members.
2. Develop assertiveness skills.
3. Develop a sense of support and cohesion, especially within the marital dyad.

## ADDITIONAL HOMEWORK THAT MAY BE APPLICABLE TO FAMILY-OF-ORIGIN INTERFERENCE

- Acting as If                                         Page 52
- How Can I Talk So He'll Listen?                      Page 89
- Why Can't You Understand My Side for Once?           Pages 164, 166
- I Am Not Jealous                                     Page 171

## ADDITIONAL PROBLEMS FOR WHICH THIS EXERCISE MAY BE USEFUL

- Communication Problems
- Jealousy/Insecurity

## SUGGESTIONS FOR PROCESSING THIS EXERCISE WITH THE CLIENT

When members of the family-of-origin interfere, the most frequent emotional reaction is frustration and anger. Oftentimes, this frustration and anger compounds, only later to become unleashed onto others unintentionally. Because such feelings can lead to resentments and conflict within the marital relationship, it is important that couples establish ways to remain unified and supportive of each other.

# HOW CAN I TELL HER TO MIND HER OWN BUSINESS?

## FOR THE COUPLE EXPERIENCING FAMILY-OF-ORIGIN INTERFERENCE WITH FAMILY ISSUES

When members of a family-of-origin interfere, the most frequent emotional reaction is frustration and anger. Oftentimes, this frustration and anger compounds, only later to become unleashed onto others unintentionally. The following exercise is designed to help you as a couple to establish ways to stay unified and supportive of each other.

1.  For the next week, make daily comments to your partner regarding how much you appreciate and care about him/her.

2.  Individually, or as a couple, identify a list of situations in which family-of-origin members interfere.

3.  At least three times over the next week, set aside quiet and alone time to express your concerns (using "I" statements) to each other, regarding the interference by family-of-origin family members.

4.  During this quiet and alone time (and preferably after having practiced in a therapy session), use role-playing techniques in front of each other to practice being assertive to an interfering family-of-origin family member.

5.  Prior to situations with family-of-origin family members who tend to interfere, review the previous role-play.

# I WANT TO GO HOME

## GOALS OF THE EXERCISE

1.  Identify thoughts and feelings about placement.
2.  Recognize and acknowledge desire for reunification.
3.  Develop action plan to achieve reunification.

## ADDITIONAL HOMEWORK THAT MAY BE APPLICABLE TO FOSTER CARE

| | |
|---|---|
| • My Safe Place | Page 19 |
| • A Picture Is Worth a Thousand Words (just pictures 1–3) | Page 215 |
| • Creating a Positive Outlook | Page 227 |

## ADDITIONAL PROBLEMS IN WHICH THIS EXERCISE MAY BE USEFUL

- Adoption
- Blended Families

## SUGGESTIONS FOR PROCESSING THIS EXERCISE WITH THE CLIENT

Foster care placement occurs for a variety of reasons. The following exercise can be used with families in which the goal is for reunification of children with family members. It is designed for children and their parent(s) or legal guardian whom they will be reunited with once out of foster care.

# I WANT TO GO HOME

This exercise is designed for families who are planning to reunite after experiencing foster care placement. The first part is only for the teens and preteens who have been in placement. The second part is for the family as a group to complete. The last part is for each member to complete individually and then to be shared with the family as a whole.

## FOR THE TEEN/PRETEEN IN FOSTER CARE TO COMPLETE

When I was placed in foster care, the reason was _____

_____

_____

My first night I felt _____ because _____

_____

Now I feel _____ about being in foster care.

I (circle) want to/do not want to be taken out of foster care and placed with _____

_____

## FOR ALL FAMILY MEMBERS TO COMPLETE

List the pros and cons to being reunited.

| Pros | Cons |
| --- | --- |
| _____ | _____ |
| _____ | _____ |
| _____ | _____ |
| _____ | _____ |
| _____ | _____ |

## FOR EACH INDIVIDUAL TO COMPLETE ABOUT HIMSELF OR HERSELF

In order for me to be united with _____

I need to do the following:

1. _____

_____

2. _____

_____

## ONE MORE IDEA

1. Identify some older adults who may have experienced foster care during their youth. Ask them if they feel that the foster care has helped them in their new life.

# WE'RE MOVING

## GOALS OF THE EXERCISE

1. Identify and express feelings regarding relocation.
2. Allow family members to be able to feel as though they have a voice in the decision.
3. Identify any alternative solutions to the relocation conflict.
4. Be able to cope effectively with the loss of friends and familiar environment.

## ADDITIONAL HOMEWORK THAT MAY BE APPLICABLE TO RELOCATING

- My Safe Place                                               Page 19
- When Can We Be Together?                                    Page 1
- The Questions, Feelings, Comments/Concerns Game            Page 102

## ADDITIONAL PROBLEMS FOR WHICH THIS EXERCISE MAY BE USEFUL

- Blended Families

## SUGGESTIONS FOR PROCESSING THIS EXERCISE WITH THE CLIENT

When a family is forced to relocate due to a parent's job, tremendous emotions usually emerge. This is especially true if family members are well-grounded (have roots) in their current community. Children—and particularly teenagers—can become quite oppositional to leaving their friends and familiar surroundings, and/or experience anxiety and depression.

One exercise that can be helpful is to instruct family members to identify and bring to the next session an object that is representative of the loss they fear about moving (e.g., student ID badge that might represent a teenager's identity). Each person must think about and describe his/her fear. The therapist is subsequently able to address the fears and help each member be heard and have their fear validated. The therapist can then help the family identify which things are negotiable and how such losses can be saved.

# WE'RE MOVING

## FOR ALL MEMBERS OF A FAMILY THAT IS EXPERIENCING RELOCATION

The following exercise can help each of you talk about the loss and associated feelings regarding the physical relocation. Before your next session, identify an object that is representative of the loss you fear about relocating. This may include student IDs or other objects that reflect a loss of standing among peers in your community, dating relationships, and so on. Each of you must think about and describe your fear and sense of loss with the move. Be prepared to discuss this in the next family session. Be sure to bring in your object.

The object I brought is _____. This represents my fear of _____

_____

_____

# SHOULD WE OR SHOULD WE NOT?

## GOALS OF THE EXERCISE

1. Have family identify the pros and cons of relocation.
2. Allow family members be able to feel as though they have a voice in the matter.
3. The family should consider possible alternatives to relocating.

## ADDITIONAL HOMEWORK THAT MAY BE APPLICABLE TO RELOCATING

## ADDITIONAL PROBLEMS FOR WHICH THIS EXERCISE MAY BE USEFUL

- Blended Families
- Family Conflict

## SUGGESTIONS FOR PROCESSING THIS EXERCISE WITH CLIENT

Oftentimes, relocating creates mixed feelings by all family members. When this occurs, family members frequently report feeling unheard. This exercise will help each family member identify his/her reasons for wanting to relocate or wanting to remain in their present domicile

# SHOULD WE OR SHOULD WE NOT?

## FOR ALL MEMBERS OF A FAMILY THAT IS CONSIDERING RELOCATION

Relocating can be an overwhelming experience. It can create many mixed emotions. The following exercise is designed to help you sort out your thoughts and feelings and to listen to everyone else's as well.

1.  As a family, record a list of the advantages and the disadvantages for moving.

| Pros | Cons |
| --- | --- |
| _____ | _____ |
| _____ | _____ |
| _____ | _____ |
| _____ | _____ |
| _____ | _____ |
| _____ | _____ |

It is important to consider any alternatives to moving, but in fairness, all family members should also convey their understanding as to why other family members view the move as necessary. To achieve these two important aspects, family members should complete the following exercise.

2.  The family members who think we should move are:

_____   _____

_____   _____

3.  List each person who thinks we should move and his/her reason.
_____ reason for moving is _____
_____
_____ reason for moving is _____
_____

_____ reason for moving is _____

_____

_____ reason for moving is _____

_____

4.  The family members who think we should NOT move are:

    _____        _____

    _____        _____

5.  List each person who thinks we should NOT move and his/her reason.
    _____ reason for NOT moving is _____

    _____

    _____ reason for NOT moving is _____

    _____

    _____ reason for NOT moving is _____

    _____

6.  I propose the following alternatives to moving:
    a. _____

    _____

    b. _____

    _____

    c. _____

    _____

## A FEW MORE IDEAS

1.  Suppose you had a best friend who came to you and informed you that they had to relocate to another area and had no choice in the matter. How would you recommend that they cope with the situation? What would your advice be to them?

    _____

    _____

2.  Identify a classmate at your present school, or a neighbor who has relocated from another area at school. Talk to them about the difficulty they experienced and how long it took before they eventually settled into this new environment. Then try to imagine how this might be applied to your own situation.

    _____

    _____

# HE ALWAYS DID LIKE YOU BEST

## GOALS OF THE EXERCISE

1. For family members to develop a sense of acceptance and understanding regarding the distribution of the will.
2. Resolve any disputes or resentments regarding the distribution of the inheritance.

## ADDITIONAL HOMEWORK THAT MAY BE APPLICABLE TO INHERITANCE DISPUTES

- How Can I Talk So He'll Listen?                  Page 89
- Why Can't You Understand My Side for Once?       Pages 164, 166

## ADDITIONAL PROBLEMS IN WHICH THIS EXERCISE MAY BE USEFUL

- Divorce Situations*

## SUGGESTIONS FOR PROCESSING THIS EXERCISE WITH THE CLIENT

The passing of a family member is typically hard no matter what the situation. Sometimes a complicating factor involves the distribution of the money and assets left behind. When a will is in place, resentments and feelings that the distribution is not equitable can further divide a family. When such problems arise during the course of family therapy, the therapist can help by providing a forum for the family members to air their differences. In addition, the therapist can structure a process for the family to resolve their resentments and feelings of unfairness.

---

*This problem is not specifically discussed in detail in this volume.

# HE ALWAYS DID LIKE YOU BEST

## FOR THE MEMBERS OF A FAMILY EXPERIENCING DISPUTES OR RESENTMENT OVER DISTRIBUTION OF A WILL

The following exercise will help each of you to identify your concerns regarding the distribution of an inheritance and express such concerns in a manner that other family members will be able to understand.

1.  As a group, or individually, develop a list of reasons for how the deceased may have arrived at his or her decision to distribute assets in the manner that was executed.

2.  When expressing your thoughts and feelings regarding the distribution, use "I" statements. These can be recorded to use in a family session where you may feel more comfortable voicing such feelings.

3.  Think about how each of your relatives may feel regarding the distribution. In the next family session, you should be prepared to acknowledge your perceptions of the feelings other members have.

4.  Think about the pros and cons of rewriting a more equitable distribution of the inheritance (e.g., I want to maintain my relationship with a loved one).

5.  Those family members interested and willing to redistribute his/her share of the inheritance should meet and discuss a more evenly distributed formula.

# THEY'RE CALLING ME A HALF-BREED

## GOALS OF THE EXERCISE

1. Learn to cope effectively with the stress of being biracial.
2. Parents and children learn to support each other.

## ADDITIONAL HOMEWORK THAT MAY BE APPLICABLE TO INTERRACIAL FAMILY PROBLEMS

| | |
|---|---|
| • I Have Too Many Parents | Page 80 |
| • Circles of Perception | Page 122 |
| • Why Can't You Understand My Side for Once? | Pages 164, 166 |

## ADDITIONAL PROBLEMS IN WHICH THIS EXERCISE MAY BE USEFUL

• Jealousy

## SUGGESTIONS FOR PROCESSING THIS EXERCISE WITH CLIENT

Interracial families frequently experience a variety of challenges and conflicts from within the family system as well as from society. These challenges and conflicts can involve the stress between parents who display some of their own hidden racial prejudices or from children who react in a resentful way toward their parents for their mixed race. Extended family members who disapprove of the interracial relationship can also create conflict and hardship. It is important that the therapist identify where these conflicts and challenges lie.

# THEY'RE CALLING ME A HALF-BREED

1. Suggest to the family that over the next week they identify the times and the associated feelings when they have each felt rejected or disapproved of for being a biracial family. You can use the sentence stem below to help family members identify and express themselves.

   I felt _____ (rejected/made fun of/ put down) because of

   being biracial when _____

   This made me think I _____

   _____

2. Tell the family to get together before the next session and describe these situations to each other. (In the next session, review these situations and have each family member express support, empathy, and respect for each other).

3. Have family members identify a list of people they feel are accepting and supportive.

   The people I feel are accepting, and support me are _____

   _____

   _____

   _____

   _____

4. Before the next session, have each family member schedule at least one activity to complete with someone on his/her list.

   The activities I would like to do include _____

   _____

   _____

   _____

   _____

   _____

   _____

5. Assign the family the task of meeting before the next session and brainstorming the pros and cons of supporting one another and identifying social supports (extended family, friends in the community/church, co-workers).

|              **Pros**              |              **Cons**              |
| ---------------------------------- | ---------------------------------- |
|                                    |                                    |
|                                    |                                    |
|                                    |                                    |
|                                    |                                    |
|                                    |                                    |
|                                    |                                    |
|                                    |                                    |

# BEFORE AND AFTER

## GOALS OF THE EXERCISE

1. Identify and increase awareness of how individual family members are perceived when intolerant or defensive.
2. Develop an understanding for how family members "could" be if they were not intolerant or defensive.
3. Develop more effective ways to respond to feeling intolerant or defensive.

## ADDITIONAL HOMEWORK THAT MAY BE APPLICABLE TO INTOLERANCE/DEFENSIVENESS

- The Blaming Jar                Page 71
- How Can I Talk So He'll Listen?     Page 89

## ADDITIONAL PROBLEMS IN WHICH THIS EXERCISE MAY BE USEFUL

- Anger Management      •     Anxiety      •     Depression

## SUGGESTIONS FOR PROCESSING THIS EXERCISE WITH FAMILY MEMBERS

Families struggling with being defensive or intolerant with each other can often be short fused. A frequent pattern of hurting each other verbally may be the norm. Oftentimes, if this has been occurring for a long period of time, family members may not know how else to act. For change to occur, awareness needs to be developed first. This exercise follows a problem resolution format and is designed to accomplish three steps. Step One is to identify the behaviors of conflict or intolerance or defensiveness. Step Two is to identify alternative behaviors. Step Three is to practice the alternative behavior.

Before the exercise is suggested, review the basic problem solving steps (i.e., define the problem narrowly, brainstorm options for solutions, generate the pros and cons of each option, select one option for implementation, implement the selected option, evaluate the results, adjust the solution as needed). Also review the use of the "stress ball" as suggested in the homework "Why Can't You Understand My Side for Once?"

# BEFORE AND AFTER

If your family struggles with being intolerant of or defensive with each other, you have learned some pretty negative interactive behaviors. These may partially involve mechanisms used in self-defense. Most families struggling with such conflict want to change but need some structure or guidelines to do it. This exercise follows a rather simple problem-solving formula to help you identify times of conflict in which defensiveness or intolerance is present. You will also be given a chance to identify and describe alternative behaviors. Finally, you are given the opportunity to practice these alternative behaviors.

Step One. Take time to notice when periods of conflict, intolerance, or defensiveness occur, and record what people are doing and saying. Use the lines below.

_____

_____

_____

_____

_____

_____

As a family, get together and describe the behaviors you recorded.

DO NOT FOCUS ON WHOM BUT RATHER ON OBSERVABLE BEHAVIORS. THE GOAL IS TO INCREASE AWARENESS OF THE BEHAVIORS/COMMENTS THAT ARE DEFENSIVE/INTOLERANT.

Step Two. As a family, try to brainstorm alternative behaviors for each defensive/intolerant behavior listed above.

_____

_____

_____

_____

_____

_____

_____

Step Three. As a family spend two to three minutes practicing these alternative behaviors.

For each family member, use an, "I" statement to describe how it feels to practice these alternative behaviors.

Using these alternative behaviors, I _____

Using these alternative behaviors, I _____

Using these alternative behaviors, I _____

Using these alternative behaviors, I _____

Using these alternative behaviors, I _____

Using these alternative behaviors, I _____

As a family, try brainstorming a list of reasons why these alternative behaviors are better than the defensive and intolerant behaviors described in Step One. Make sure each family member offers at least one reason.

These alternative behaviors are better for our family because:

_____

_____

_____

_____

_____

_____

_____

_____

_____

Throughout the week remind each other and yourself of these reasons.

# WHY CAN'T YOU UNDERSTAND MY SIDE FOR ONCE? (PART I)

## GOALS OF THE EXERCISE

1. To reduce and possibly eliminate the tension and conflict regarding the attitudes of self-righteousness and superiority over others.
2. Become more open-minded and tolerant of one another.

## ADDITIONAL HOMEWORK THAT MAY BE APPLICABLE TO INTOLERANCE/DEFENSIVENESS

- The Blaming Jar      Page 71
- How Can I Talk So He'll Listen?      Page 89
- Why Can't You Understand My Side for Once? (Part II)      Page 166

## ADDITIONAL PROBLEMS FOR WHICH THIS EXERCISE MAY BE USEFUL

- Anger
- Anxiety
- Depression

## SUGGESTIONS FOR PROCESSING THIS EXERCISE WITH CLIENT

Attitudes of self-righteousness and superiority naturally create distance between individuals and can lead to resentment as well as end relationships. A family who is looking to prevent such consequences will need to identify the behaviors that family members engage in when these attitudes are evident. They will also need to identify the thoughts and feelings that these episodes instill. Additionally, all of this needs to be discussed as a family. It is important for family members to define what type of family life they want to have and what this would look like. Typically the first step in this process is helping the family members to identify and acknowledge each others' thoughts and feelings.

# WHY CAN'T YOU UNDERSTAND MY SIDE FOR ONCE? (PART I)

## FOR THE MEMBERS OF A FAMILY THAT IS EXPERIENCING INTERNAL PROBLEMS WITH INTOLERANCE AND DEFENSIVENESS

As a family agree on, and commit to, a time within the next week when you can meet and complete the following activity:

1. Each family member is to identify a rather neutral issue and present his or her view of it. For example, one member can describe how he or she enjoys ice skating.

2. Each family member then expresses agreement and understanding (regarding, for example, how his/her sibling or parent enjoys ice skating).

3. The family should record, or at least make a mental note of, the following:

   a. How s/he felt and thought when expressing his or her neutral issue.

   b. How s/he felt and thought when the others expressed acknowledgment and understanding.

   c. How s/he felt and thought when it was her or his turn to express acknowledgment and understanding.

# WHY CAN'T YOU UNDERSTAND MY SIDE FOR ONCE? (PART II)

## GOALS OF THE EXERCISE

1. Identify the roadblocks to talking without arguing.
2. Develop effective ways to talk with each other without arguing.

## ADDITIONAL HOMEWORK THAT MAY BE APPLICABLE TO INTOLERANCE/DEFENSIVENESS

- The Blaming Jar                           Page 71
- How Can I Talk So He'll Listen?       Page 89
- Why Can't You Understand My Side for Once? (Part I)     Page 164

## ADDITIONAL PROBLEMS IN WHICH THIS EXERCISE MAY BE USEFUL

- Anger
- Communication Problems

## SUGGESTIONS FOR PROCESSING THIS EXERCISE WITH THE CLIENT

When family members cannot get their point across because of constant arguing, it is important to identify the process that is occurring (e.g., talking over each other, ignoring). In a session, the therapist can work with the family to identify these ineffective strategies and then to help implement signals or other ways to identify and interrupt this process. For example, when family members are talking over each other, assign a rule that the only one who can talk is the one with the "stress ball" in his/her hand. It may also be helpful to set a time limit (such as 1 or 2 minutes), after which the ball goes to another family member. This ball may also be substituted for a piece of linoleum, as in the exercise introduced by Markman, Stanley, and Blumberg (1994) of "Who Has the Floor?" or the use of "The Pad and Pencil Technique" (Dattilio, 2007), or "Passing the Hat" with families (Dattilio, 1994).

# WHY CAN'T YOU UNDERSTAND MY SIDE FOR ONCE? (PART II)

This exercise should be attempted after you and your therapist have discussed and practiced strategies for managing conversations (e.g., use of a piece of linoleum to indicate who has the floor to speak) and deep breathing.

1.  At home, family members can practice having conversations using the signals and strategies (e.g., linoleum) developed in the therapy session.

2.  Family members should also practice deep breathing as a way to manage their feelings. You can visualize a thermometer, which will record the level of your feelings. When the thermometer is close to indicating a fever, practice deep breathing.

3.  Sometimes when an individual cannot break his or her fever, a time-out is needed. When you need to take a time-out, try to set a time limit (such as 10 minutes). In using a time-out, it is important that an attempt be made to continue the conversation. If this cannot be done, the topic should be discussed in the next session, where your therapist can help bring closure to the conversation.

# I DON'T HAVE TO BE JEALOUS
# OR INSECURE ANYMORE

## GOALS OF THE EXERCISE

1. Identify and increase awareness of controlling behaviors within the family.
2. Develop an understanding for the need to be in control.
3. Reduce the fear or identify the insecurity that often drives the need to be in control.
4. Decrease frustration of family members.

## ADDITIONAL HOMEWORK THAT MAY BE APPLICABLE TO CLIENTS WITH JEALOUSY/INSECURITY

- How Can I Talk So He'll Listen?                  Page 89
- Why Can't You Understand My Side for Once?       Pages 164, 166

## ADDITIONAL PROBLEMS IN WHICH THIS EXERCISE MAY BE USEFUL

- Oppositional
- Defiant Behavior
- Parent/Child Conflict
- Relationship Conflict

## SUGGESTIONS FOR PROCESSING THIS EXERCISE WITH THE CLIENT

When individuals feel jealous, they may often try to be controlling of others. This controlling behavior can take many different forms such as snide comments, sarcasm, silences, or unjust punishments. Jealousy and insecurity can often be driven by a fear that the person believes will come true if they don't control the situation. The following exercise is designed to identify the controlling behavior as well as the fear.

# I DON'T HAVE TO BE JEALOUS
# OR INSECURE ANYMORE

During the session, family members are to make a list of controlling behaviors that are often displayed within the home. This should be done without necessarily identifying who typically engages in that behavior. A family member can be in charge of writing this list of controlling behaviors and posting it somewhere in the home as a reminder to all members. This is often placed on the refrigerator. The following steps make up this homework assignment.

1. Step One is for a family member to post the list of controlling behaviors typically displayed within the home.

2. Step Two is to take note of any time a controlling behavior is displayed. Family members can record this on a note pad and put it in a jar or container. These notes will be used for Step Three.

3. Step Three is to meet as a family and discuss possible reasons the family member was acting in a controlling fashion. Use the lines below to brainstorm possible reasons. It is generally more productive if the family works to identify reasons to understand why a person was controlling as opposed to making an angry list of put-downs and complaints.

   An example could be, "He was telling me what to do to help me. When he 'helps' me it makes him feel included. Being included is important to him."

   _____

   _____

   _____

4. Step Four is for the family to acknowledge the controlling person's fear. For example, "I won't be included." Use the incomplete sentences below to identify and express any fears that the controlling person has.

   I understand that _____ (e.g., you want to be included).

   I understand that _____

   I understand that _____

5. Step Five involves providing reassurance to reduce the controlling person's fear.

6. For example, "I know you want to be involved and want to help me. Let me know your ideas. I'll listen and can then make an informed decision." Use the lines below to write some reassuring comments or phrases.

_____

_____

_____

In the next session, review this homework and have the family role-play a corrective experience. This could involve the controlling person catching him or herself and changing their behavior. Other family members can then offer reassuring comments and praise for making change.

# I AM NOT JEALOUS

## GOALS OF THE EXERCISE

1. Reduce and/or eliminate feelings of jealousy/insecurity.
2. Eliminate blaming of each other regarding overt or perceived favoritism.

## ADDITIONAL HOMEWORK THAT MAY BE APPLICABLE
## TO JEALOUSY/INSECURITY

- How Can I Talk So He Will Listen?           Page 89
- Why Can't You Understand My Side for Once?    Pages 164, 166

## ADDITIONAL PROBLEMS FOR WHICH THIS EXERCISE MAY BE USEFUL

- Anger Problems
- Anxiety
- Depression
- Selfishness*

## SUGGESTIONS FOR PROCESSING THIS EXERCISE WITH THE CLIENT

Feelings of jealousy and insecurity can lead to very intense conflicts within family relationships. At times, a dependency ensues, leaving family members feeling trapped in a cycle. Other family members who observe the jealous and dependent behavior frequently become resentful and angry. Explain to family members their cycle and how destructive it can become. Once they have agreed to make some changes, provide them with the following exercise.

---

*This problem is not specifically discussed in detail in this volume.

# I AM NOT JEALOUS

## FOR THE MEMBERS OF A FAMILY THAT IS EXPERIENCING FEELINGS OF JEALOUSY/INSECURITY

Feelings of jealousy and insecurity can lead to very intense conflicts within family relationships. The following exercise is designed to help you reduce or eliminate feelings of jealousy/insecurity as well as the blaming of each other regarding perceived or overt favoritism.

1.  Identify what each of you believes to be the insecure and/or jealous behavior.

    I believe the jealous/insecure behavior is _____

    _____

    _____

    I believe the jealous/insecure behavior is _____

    _____

    _____

    I believe the jealous/insecure behavior is _____

    _____

    _____

    I believe the jealous/insecure behavior is _____

    _____

    _____

    I believe the jealous/insecure behavior is _____

    _____

    _____

    I believe the jealous/insecure behavior is _____

    _____

    _____

    I believe the jealous/insecure behavior is _____

    _____

    _____

I believe the jealous/insecure behavior is _____

_____

_____

2. Identify the thoughts that come to your mind when you observe these behaviors of jealousy.

When I see that jealous behavior, I think _____

_____

_____

When I see that jealous behavior, I think _____

_____

_____

When I see that jealous behavior, I think _____

_____

_____

When I see that jealous behavior, I think _____

_____

_____

When I see that jealous behavior, I think _____

_____

_____

When I see that jealous behavior, I think _____

_____

_____

3. Identify a list of alternative thoughts or actions, which can replace episodes of jealousy or insecurity. If you are having trouble, ask other family members for some input.

An alternative thought could be _____

_____

_____

An alternative thought could be _____

_____

_____

An alternative thought could be _____

_____

_____

An alternative thought could be _____

_____

_____

An alternative thought could be _____

_____

_____

An alternative thought could be _____

_____

_____

4. Practice taking a deep breath during situations in which you observe jealous/insecure behavior, and think about the benefits of the alternative thoughts and/or actions.

# JOHNNY HAS LEUKEMIA

## GOALS OF THE EXERCISE

1. For family members to open up lines of communication regarding the terminal or chronic illness of one or more members.
2. To identify the primary areas of stress within the family and assess its effects.
3. To develop stress-reduction techniques and maintain or create a supportive family and social support network.

## ADDITIONAL HOMEWORK THAT MAY BE APPLICABLE TO LIFE-THREATENING/CHRONIC ILLNESS

- What Do Others Value about Me?          Page 117
- Why Is Dad in Bed All Day?              Page 183

## ADDITIONAL PROBLEMS FOR WHICH THIS EXERCISE MAY BE USEFUL

- Family Conflicts*     • Physical Disabilities     • Single Parenting*

## SUGGESTIONS FOR PROCESSING THIS EXERCISE WITH CLIENT

A life-threatening or chronic illness is often devastating, especially when it strikes a younger member or more than one member of the family. It is important for family members to be familiar with the various stages they will face with the progress of the illness (i.e., shock, denial, and grief). It is also important that family members identify and express the thoughts and feelings they are experiencing. Oftentimes, it is helpful to identify a social support network. During the course of treatment, most families are dealing with issues such as stress, guilt, and depression regarding their son/daughter or parent or other relative who may be afflicted. The following exercise is designed to help families (including the member with the life-threatening chronic illness) to identify ways to reduce tension and stress.

---

*These problems are not specifically discussed in detail in this volume.

# JOHNNY HAS LEUKEMIA

## FOR THE MEMBERS OF A FAMILY EXPERIENCING A LIFE-THREATENING OR CHRONIC ILLNESS

The following exercise will help you as a family open up the lines of communication regarding the terminal or chronic illness. After completing the exercise, you should feel greater support from one another.

1. Each family member is to identify situations that create feelings of stress or conflict. Utilize "I" statements to facilitate a safe and nonthreatening atmosphere. For example, "I feel really stressed out when I have to cook dinner, clean up the dishes, and get ready to go visit Johnny in the hospital. I would feel calmer and would act more pleasant if everyone could pitch in and help."

2. Each family member is to identify what worries him/her the most about _____'s chronic illness.

3. Each family member is to describe for the others the situations that create stress for him or her.

4. Each family member is to identify and express the positive feelings they have toward one another. The more reminders, the better.

5. As a group, family members are to brainstorm ways in which they can reduce feelings of stress. To generate even more ideas, have them ask other family members or friends how they cope.

6. All family members need to stay in touch with their own level of stress (e.g., stress thermometer, or numerical rating 1 to 10) and identify at what level they need to practice deep breathing, taking a walk, working on a fun hobby/activity, asking for a hug, calling a friend, and so forth.

7. Community support groups that are comprised of other families with chronically ill members may also be something to try.

# WITH SEVEN YOU GET AN EGGROLL

## GOALS OF THE EXERCISE

1. Express thoughts and feelings regarding the birth of multiple children.
2. Identify stress management techniques to deal with the obligations and burdens of having multiple children.
3. Identify resources available and needed (physical, emotional, financial) to assist in childcare.

## ADDITIONAL HOMEWORK THAT MAY BE APPLICABLE TO MULTIPLE-BIRTH DILEMMAS

- When I Feel Anxious It Is Like . . .         Page 42

## ADDITIONAL PROBLEMS FOR WHICH THIS EXERCISE MAY BE USEFUL

- Unwanted/Unplanned Pregnancies

## SUGGESTIONS FOR PROCESSING THIS EXERCISE WITH CLIENT

The birth of a child is a wondrous and miraculous event. Experiencing the birth of several at a time is even more miraculous but can be quite overwhelming as well. All members in the family will need to identify and express their feelings as the dichotomy of joy and stress abound.

# WITH SEVEN YOU GET AN EGGROLL

## FOR THE MEMBERS OF A FAMILY EXPERIENCING MULTIPLE BIRTHS

The birth of a child is a wondrous and miraculous event. Experiencing the birth of several at a time is even more miraculous but can be quite overwhelming as well. All members in the family will need to identify and express their feelings as the dichotomy of joy and stress abound.

1.  Family members should first freely express their shock and fears with each other regarding being able to handle such responsibilities. (Try to use as many "I" statements as possible.)

2.  As a group discuss various ways of handling stress. (Perhaps listing these ideas and putting the list where it can be easily accessed would be beneficial.) Typically with stress, individuals will engage in various types of negative self-talk. Such talk should be identified and replaced by positive and realistic statements.

3.  Write a list of any negative statements. Additional statements can be added.

4.  Write an alternative list that counters each negative statement. These two lists should be kept in plain view or easily accessible.

# HOW ARE WE GOING TO DO THIS?

## GOALS OF THE EXERCISE

1. To reduce the level of stress that families will inevitably feel when experiencing simultaneous multiple births.
2. To identify ways of adjusting to the new family size and to the numerous responsibilities that accompany the births.

## ADDITIONAL HOMEWORK THAT MAY BE APPLICABLE TO MULTIPLE-BIRTH DILEMMAS

- When I Feel Anxious It Is Like . . .          Page 42

## ADDITIONAL PROBLEMS FOR WHICH THIS EXERCISE MAY BE USEFUL

- Unwanted/Unplanned Pregnancies

## SUGGESTIONS FOR PROCESSING THIS EXERCISE WITH CLIENT

Families experiencing simultaneous multiple births will need to make many decisions regarding living arrangements, who can help and when, where will they get the clothes and food for their new babies, how will they pay for it all, and many others. Adjusting will require a significant amount of effort and energy as well as the support of others.

# HOW ARE WE GOING TO DO THIS?

## FOR THE MEMBERS OF A FAMILY EXPERIENCING MULTIPLE BIRTHS

It is tough enough for couples to have one child. The birth of multiple children increases such struggles and worries. This exercise will help you create some strategies for coping with the many stresses that accompany multiple childbirths.

1. Contact the nearest support group and attend two or three meetings.

2. Pull together other family members as well as friends who are willing to help out. Discuss what help is needed and at what times. Also, designate who in the family will coordinate these efforts.

3. Develop a daily schedule of who is doing what and when. Be sure that you include lighthearted family recreational activities at least every other week, or at least a weekly family meeting to discuss how each person is doing.

# KNOWING WHAT TO EXPECT

## GOALS OF THE EXERCISE

1. To establish a daily routine for a child experiencing a pervasive developmental disorder.
2. To provide structure and security for the child.

## ADDITIONAL HOMEWORK THAT MAY BE APPLICABLE TO PERVASIVE DEVELOPMENTAL DISORDER

- Charting Our Course          Page 58

## ADDITIONAL PROBLEMS FOR WHICH THIS EXERCISE MAY BE USEFUL

- Mental Retardation*

## SUGGESTIONS FOR PROCESSING THIS EXERCISE WITH THE CLIENT

Children with pervasive developmental disorders require a great deal of structure and consistency in their daily life. When change occurs (even in transitioning from one activity to another), problems of acting-out behavior such as yelling, screaming, and/or hitting can occur. In order to reduce the frequency of such behaviors, it is helpful to design a daily routine. It is also helpful to include visual aids so that the child can see himself/herself doing each activity.

---

*This problem is not specifically discussed in detail in this volume.

# KNOWING WHAT TO EXPECT

## FOR THE PARENTS OF A CHILD WITH A PERVASIVE DEVELOPMENTAL DISORDER

A child with a pervasive developmental disorder requires a great deal of structure and consistency in his/her daily life. When change occurs (even in transitioning from one activity to another), problems of acting-out behavior such as yelling, screaming, and/or hitting can occur. In order to reduce the frequency of such behaviors it is helpful to design a daily routine. It is also helpful to include visual aids so that your child can see himself or herself doing each activity. The following activity will help you get started toward creating a daily routine.

1.  Make a chart identifying the activities your child generally engages in, and the corresponding times. For example:

    |  | **Monday** |
    |------|------|
    | 7:45 | Wakes up |
    | 8:00 | Gets dressed |
    | 8:15 | Eats breakfast |
    | 8:45 | Takes bus to school |

2.  Next to each activity and time, put a photograph of your child doing that activity. Or, have your child draw a picture of him or herself doing that activity.

# WHY IS DAD IN BED ALL DAY?

## GOALS OF THE EXERCISE

1. For family members to open up lines of communication regarding the health problems affecting one of the members.
2. To prevent or reduce the distance as well as enmeshment that develops within family relationships.
3. Identify and express thoughts and feelings regarding the disability.

## ADDITIONAL HOMEWORK THAT MAY BE APPLICABLE TO PHYSICAL DISABILITIES

- How Can I Talk So He'll Listen?           Page 89
- What Do Others Value about Me?           Page 117
- Johnny Has Leukemia                        Page 175

## ADDITIONAL PROBLEMS FOR WHICH THIS EXERCISE MAY BE USEFUL

- Blended Families
- Life-Threatening/Chronic Illnesses

## SUGGESTIONS FOR PROCESSING THIS EXERCISE WITH THE CLIENT

Families who have a member with a chronic physical or mental disability oftentimes will experience a range of emotions such as confusion, anger, resentment, guilt, and/or sadness. Many times, family members prefer not to talk much about their feelings and thoughts regarding how the disabled member is affecting them. It is also typical for family members to not talk with the member who is disabled regarding such feelings. As a result, these thoughts and feelings remain tucked away without much room for an outlet. In families who have a disabled member, it is important for a therapist to explore feelings.

In a family session the therapist should bring the topic of physical disabilities to light and process any fears or concerns with regard to discussing the issue. This may be difficult because it may be a family secret in the sense that "we don't talk about that topic." Once the therapist is able to get the family to a point of agreement that this topic needs to be discussed, suggest the following homework assignment.

# WHY IS DAD IN BED ALL DAY?

## FOR THE MEMBERS OF A FAMILY EXPERIENCING A DISABILITY

This exercise will help you as a family to open up the lines of communication regarding each others' thoughts and feelings about the disability.

1. Each family member is to think about and write down his/her own perceptions and understanding of what the disability involves (e.g., What is it called? How long will it last? Will it get any worse or better? What is the treatment for it?).

2. Identify the thoughts and feelings that each of you has when you think about the disability.

3. As a family, schedule a time to meet and discuss your responses to item 1. If this is too difficult, have the family members bring their responses and questions to the next counseling session to be processed with the therapist.

4. Schedule a weekly family meeting or activity to decrease any isolation of the family member with the disability and to reinforce a sense of family unity.

**Therapist's Overview**

# WHAT IS OKAY AND WHAT IS NOT OKAY?

## GOALS OF THE EXERCISE

1. Family members identify and define what is abusive or inappropriate.
2. The family will develop a list of alternatives to abusive behavior.

## ADDITIONAL HOMEWORK THAT MAY BE APPLICABLE TO PHYSICAL, VERBAL, PSYCHOLOGICAL ABUSE

- My Safe Place                                      Page 19
- Is It Passive, Aggressive, or Assertive?           Page 21
- Acting as If                                       Page 52
- How Can I Talk So He'll Listen?                    Page 89

## ADDITIONAL PROBLEMS IN WHICH THIS EXERCISE MAY BE USEFUL

- Blame
- Dependency
- Jealousy/Insecurity

## SUGGESTIONS FOR PROCESSING THIS EXERCISE WITH CLIENT

It is generally very difficult to discuss abuse or inappropriate behaviors that are present within a family. Family members are oftentimes reluctant to discuss abuse for fear of retaliation. If a family is ready to deal with this issue, they will need some guidelines and support. The following exercise is designed to provide some guidelines for the family to first define what behavior is not okay and secondly to identify what is okay. In some situations, this exercise could help initiate a discussion regarding abusive or inappropriate interactions.

# WHAT IS OKAY AND WHAT IS NOT OKAY?

This exercise is intended to help you discuss types of family interactions/behaviors and allow individual family members to express their thoughts and feelings. It is intended for the family to come to an agreement on what is okay and not okay and why. The exercise will also help you to identify how you as a family would prefer to interact.

Take a look at the following list. Each family member is to identify which behaviors you would like to experience and which behaviors you prefer not to experience.

Use the additional lines to record other behaviors.

Being given a compliment.

Receiving a hug.

Being physically hit by another family member.

Being called names or put down by a family member.

A family member asking for your help.

Being told thank you.

A family member threatening to hurt you or damage something that is yours.

A family member ignoring you or refusing to talk with you.

_____

_____

_____

_____

_____

_____

_____

Make a list of the behaviors you do not want to experience. Each family member is to identify reasons why these behaviors are not wanted.

Behaviors we don't want in our family!

_____

_____

_____

_____
_____
_____
_____
_____
_____
_____
_____

These behaviors are not wanted because:

_____
_____
_____
_____
_____
_____
_____
_____
_____
_____

Now that you have agreed to what you don't want and have identified why, work together and identify a list of alternatives to the abusive or inappropriate behaviors.

The behaviors and interactions we want in our family are:

_____
_____
_____
_____
_____
_____
_____
_____
_____
_____
_____
_____

# I DON'T KNOW WHAT TO BELIEVE IN ANYMORE

## GOALS OF THE EXERCISE

1. Family members will be able to resolve interfaith conflicts.
2. Parents will be able to agree on child-rearing practices.

## ADDITIONAL HOMEWORK THAT MAY BE APPLICABLE TO RELIGIOUS/SPIRITUAL CONFLICTS

- How Can I Talk So He'll Listen?                    Page 89
- Circles of Perception                               Page 122
- Why Can't You Understand My Side for Once?         Pages 164, 166

## ADDITIONAL PROBLEMS FOR WHICH THIS EXERCISE MAY BE USEFUL

- Geographic Relocation

## SUGGESTIONS FOR PROCESSING THIS EXERCISE WITH CLIENT

Religious conflicts often have a negative effect on child-rearing practices and can become a central point of contention within the marriage. As a result, children and adolescents will often reject both parents' religious faith/beliefs and refuse to participate in any services.

# I DON'T KNOW WHAT TO BELIEVE IN ANYMORE

This exercise will help you in achieving some resolution to interfaith conflicts. You will need to meet as a family and be willing to listen to each other's comments and points of view.

1.  As a family, construct a list of reasons to respect each person's religious faith/ beliefs.

    I should respect _____ religious faith/beliefs because:

    _____

    _____

    _____

    _____

    _____

    _____

    _____

    _____

2.  As a family, brainstorm a list of the pros and cons for continuing to be in conflict (Why we should continue to be conflicted? Why we should resolve this conflict?).

| **Continue in Conflict** | **Resolve the Conflict** |
| --- | --- |
| _____ | _____ |
| _____ | _____ |
| _____ | _____ |
| _____ | _____ |
| _____ | _____ |
| _____ | _____ |

3.  Discuss the pros and cons of taking turns participating in both religions on a regular basis.

| Pros | Cons |
|------|------|
| _____ | _____ |
| _____ | _____ |
| _____ | _____ |
| _____ | _____ |
| _____ | _____ |
| _____ | _____ |

4.  Each member could attend a service of the other's denomination in order to achieve a better understanding for each other's faith.

# MY BROTHER HEARS VOICES

## GOALS OF THE EXERCISE

1. Identify thoughts and feelings regarding having a parent/spouse who hears voices.
2. Be able to express such thoughts and feelings.
3. For the family member experiencing the voices, to express his/her thoughts and feelings.

## ADDITIONAL HOMEWORK THAT MAY BE APPLICABLE TO SCHIZOPHRENIA

* My Safe Place                   Page 19
* Creating a Positive Outlook     Page 227

## ADDITIONAL PROBLEMS FOR WHICH THIS EXERCISE MAY BE USEFUL

* Anger
* Depression

## SUGGESTIONS FOR PROCESSING THIS EXERCISE WITH THE CLIENT

Having a parent or family member who suffers from hallucinations can be very scary and confusing, not to mention stressful to everyone. Oftentimes, this can be a family secret, which everyone knows about but never discusses. Even after a family is able to acknowledge that this is happening, talking about it can still be difficult. The following exercise is designed to assist family members in discussing their thoughts and feelings about this issue.

# MY BROTHER HEARS VOICES

The following exercise will help you to discuss your thoughts and feelings regarding the family member who is hearing voices.

## FOR THOSE WHO HAVE A SPOUSE OR FAMILY MEMBER WHO HEARS VOICES

1.  Describe what your understanding is of someone who hears voices (describe what it might be like or why you think it happens).

    _____

    _____

    _____

    _____

2.  When do you notice when your _____ is hearing voices? How can you tell?

    _____

    _____

    _____

    _____

3.  What do you do when your _____ is hearing voices?

    _____

    _____

    _____

4.  What things do you worry about when your _____ is hearing voices?

    _____

    _____

    _____

5.  What other thoughts and feelings do you have about your _____ hearing voices? _____

    _____

_____

6.  In what way would you like things to be different?

_____

_____

## FOR THE FAMILY MEMBER WHO IS HEARING THE VOICES

1.  Describe what it is like for you when you are hearing voices.

_____

_____

_____

2.  What things do you worry about when you are hearing voices?

_____

_____

3.  What other thoughts and feelings do you have about hearing voices?

_____

_____

_____

4.  How does your family feel about you and about you hearing voices?

_____

_____

_____

5.  How do you feel about your family's feelings?

_____

_____

_____

# MY TEENAGER IS TRUANT

## GOALS OF THE EXERCISE

1. Parents vent their feelings of disappointment and frustration.
2. Parents verbalize the reasons for their expectations for son/daughter to succeed in school.
3. Parents identify their fears of son/daughter not succeeding in school.
4. Parents identify some of their own failed accomplishments that may be contributing to their frustration.
5. Identify triggers to wanting to avoid school or certain classes.
6. Identify alternative ways of coping by reviewing coping skills.
7. Increase the amount of time in school.

## ADDITIONAL HOMEWORK THAT MAY BE APPLICABLE TO CLIENTS WITH TRUANCY PROBLEMS

- Acting as If                        Page 52
- Should We or Should We Not?          Page 153

## ADDITIONAL PROBLEMS FOR WHICH THIS EXERCISE MAY BE USEFUL

- Addictions                              • Unwanted/Unplanned Pregnancy
- Oppositional Defiant Behavior*

## SUGGESTIONS FOR PROCESSING THIS EXERCISE WITH THE CLIENT

This exercise is designed for students not attending class or school regularly. Meet with the student, parent(s), or school staff to discuss strategies attempted. The student may be experiencing: addiction, depression, anxiety, physical disability, and/or learning deficiency. Issues that apply should be addressed in the treatment plan. Parents should do their assignment first and schedule a session to discuss their responses. The student should then do their assignment and discuss responses in a session. Questions regarding substance abuse, depression, and anxiety should be discussed at both sessions. A family session should be held to discuss results and impressions at previous sessions.

---

*This problem is not specifically discussed in detail in this volume.

# MY TEENAGER IS TRUANT

## FOR THE PARENTS

Please respond to the following questions before the next appointment.

1. What are my/our expectations of my/our son/daughter (e.g., I expect my son to maintain at least a "C" average and attend all classes on a daily basis)? Would I classify these expectations as realistic or unrealistic?

   a. _____

   _____

   b. _____

   _____

   c. _____

   _____

2. What may be some of the reasons for my/our son/daughter doing poorly in school? Here, parents should be encouraged to think in behavioral terms instead of personality traits (e.g., She does not do any homework versus she is lazy). When these are discussed in a parent session, the possibility of substance use, depression, medical problems, learning difficulties, and so on, should be considered.

   a. _____

   _____

   b. _____

   _____

   c. _____

   _____

3. What is your worst fear about your son/daughter not succeeding in school? Describe how it may have an impact on all members of the family. How will those who are important to you view you as a parent and as a person?

   a. _____

   _____

b. _____
   _____
c. _____
   _____

## FOR THE STUDENT(S)

Please respond to the following questions before your next session.

1. What am I doing, as well as not doing, that may be causing me to do poorly in school?

    a. _____
    b. _____
    c. _____
    d. _____

2. How would my life be different if I were to improve my academic and behavioral performance?

    a. _____
       _____
    b. _____
       _____
    c. _____
       _____
    d. _____
       _____

3. What would I need to do in order to improve my performance in school (e.g., have more of a positive attitude, do more homework, decrease the amount of time that I spend fooling around)?

    a. _____
    b. _____
    c. _____
    d. _____

4. What would my life be like if I did not have to attend school?

    a. _____
       _____

b. _____

_____

c. _____

_____

d. _____

_____

5. If I truly do not care about school, then what are some of my alternatives?

a. _____

b. _____

c. _____

d. _____

6. How might my life be affected in the future if I were to fail out of school?

a. _____

_____

b. _____

_____

c. _____

_____

d. _____

_____

7. Why should I do better in school?

a. _____

_____

_____

b. _____

_____

_____

c. _____

_____

_____

d. _____

_____

_____

# MY PARENTS ARE GETTING A DIVORCE

## GOALS OF THE EXERCISE

1. Each member of the family expresses his or her fears about the family breakup. "We're no longer the family I knew." "I'll lose my mom/dad/brother/sister."
2. Help each family member define his or her role within the family. "Where do I fit in now that things have changed?"
3. Help family members identify when limits or boundaries are being broken.
4. Discuss the fears that children may have about their parents finding new spouses or moving the family to another location.

## ADDITIONAL HOMEWORK THAT MAY BE APPLICABLE TO DIVORCE/SEPARATION

- My Safe Place                                               Page 19
- A Picture Is Worth a Thousand Words (just pictures 1–3)      Page 215
- Creating a Positive Outlook                                  Page 227

## ADDITIONAL PROBLEMS IN WHICH THIS EXERCISE MAY BE USEFUL

- Blended Families
- Death/Loss Issues
- Foster Care
- Geographic Relocation

## SUGGESTIONS FOR PROCESSING THIS EXERCISE WITH THE CLIENT

This exercise is designed to help teens and preteens express their thoughts and feelings regarding their parents' separation or divorce.

## ONE MORE IDEA

Suggest the use of certain reading materials, such as:

*Dinosaur's Divorce* (for children under 10) (Brown & Brown, 1998)

*Children Are Not Divorceable* (Bonkowski, 1990a)

*Teens Are Not Divorceable* (Bonkowski, 1990b)

# MY PARENTS ARE GETTING A DIVORCE

## FOR TEENS/PRETEENS WHOSE PARENTS ARE DIVORCING

Write a letter, using the following questions and incomplete sentence blanks, to describe your thoughts and feelings regarding your parents' separation and how things might be after (or now that) they have separated.

1.  I think my parents should not be separated because:

    _____

    _____

    _____

2.  I think they should be separated because:

    _____

    _____

    _____

3.  Describe at least one thing you remember that you like and at least one thing that you do not care for about each family member.

    _____

    _____

    _____

    _____

4.  What I remember most about my family as a whole (before my parents decided to separate) was:

    _____

    _____

    _____

5.  The worst thing about my parents getting a divorce or being separated is:

    _____

    _____

_____

_____

6. One of the things I notice that is different about my family now that my parents are separated (or now that my parents have told me that they plan to get a divorce) is:

_____

_____

_____

7. What I like about the way things are now is:

_____

_____

_____

_____

8. What I do not like about the way things are now is:

_____

_____

_____

_____

# I WILL BE A SURVIVOR!

## GOALS OF THE EXERCISE

1. To increase a sense of being a survivor and decrease or eliminate a sense of being a victim.
2. Help family members support each other by discussing the effects of the abuse.

## ADDITIONAL HOMEWORK THAT MAY BE APPLICABLE TO ANXIETY

- My Safe Place                                         Page 19
- Acting as If                                          Page 52
- What Am I Thinking When I Am Feeling Depressed?       Page 115

## ADDITIONAL PROBLEMS IN WHICH THIS EXERCISE MAY BE USEFUL

- Anger Management
- Domestic Violence
- Physical/Verbal/Psychological Abuse
- Separation/Divorce
- Traumatic Experiences

## SUGGESTIONS FOR PROCESSING THIS EXERCISE WITH THE CLIENT

This exercise can help create a forum for which family members can identify and express their thoughts and feelings regarding their reactions to the abuse. All family members are affected when one member is abused. Everyone becomes a victim and all can become survivors. This exercise can help create unity and support within the family. It can also be used to help prevent the abuse from being swept under the rug. Avoiding the elephant in the room will exacerbate the feelings and can promote emotional distance. Not talking about the abuse can reinforce the idea that the abuse is too scary or bad to talk about. This can cause additional emotional trauma to the member who was abused.

# I WILL BE A SURVIVOR!

When a family member is abused, it affects the entire family. As a family unit, all individuals go through a process of healing. The person abused will obviously have a more difficult journey, and therefore support is essential. One way to provide support is for each member to discuss what s/he needs to move from victim to survivor. In doing so, family members can be made aware of what each person needs and can offer support. Talking openly about this journey of healing also empowers each member and helps each member realize that they are not alone. Be careful not to compare who has the toughest journey. The hardest problem to solve is whichever problem you are dealing with.

The following exercise is intended to provide each family member with an opportunity to tell his/her story and identify how they can move from feeling like a victim to feeling like a survivor.

## FOR THE FAMILY MEMBER WHO WAS ABUSED

At what point did the abuse cease?

_____

_____

_____

_____

How did the abuse stop?

_____

_____

_____

_____

What were your thoughts about it?

_____

_____

_____

_____

_____

How has the abuse affected your life with regard to:

Friends:

_____

_____

_____

Going out and being social:

_____

_____

_____

Being alone:

_____

_____

_____

Sense of safety:

_____

_____

_____

Sense of self-worth or self-esteem:

_____

_____

_____

Sense of trust in self:

_____

_____

_____

Sense of trust in others:

_____

_____

_____

Do you ever fear that you will become abusive to someone else?

## FOR NONABUSED FAMILY MEMBERS

How did you learn of the abuse?

_____

_____

_____

_____

_____

What were your thoughts?

_____

_____

_____

_____

_____

How has it affected you with regard to:

Wanting/needing to protect the family member who was abused:

_____

_____

_____

Your view of yourself:

_____

_____

_____

Your relationship with the family member who was abused:

_____

_____

_____

## FOR ALL FAMILY MEMBERS

What about the abuse makes you feel:

Angry?

_____

_____

_____

Sad?

_____

_____

_____

Confused?

_____

_____

_____

Scared?

_____

_____

_____

When someone in the family has been abused, it affects all family members in one way or the other. All family members become victimized. All can also become survivors. One of the most important decisions to be made is to accept that responsibility for the abuse lies with the perpetrator and only the perpetrator. Blaming oneself will keep you in the shoes of a victim. There are also many other ways in which one can remain in the shoes of the victim.

See if as a family, you can generate a list of ways one can remain a victim.

Blaming self _____

Focus on the past or on the abuse _____

Feeling hopeless _____

Not trusting _____

"Woulda, coulda, shoulda" thoughts _____

_____

_____

_____

_____

_____

_____

_____

Now make a list of ways one can **be a survivor**.

<u>Gaining sense of trust in self and others</u>

<u>Feeling empowered</u>

<u>Focusing on the future and the positives</u>

<u>Holding perpetrator responsible</u>

<u>Engaged in one's life and interests/hobbies</u>

_____

_____

_____

_____

_____

_____

Make a list of why you want to be a survivor and NOT a victim.

_____

_____

_____

_____

_____

_____

_____

_____

_____

_____

_____

_____

_____

_____

Make a commitment to each other to support and encourage each other to be a survivor. Remind each other of the reasons being a survivor is better.

# GETTING IT OUT

## GOALS OF THE EXERCISE

1. To begin a process of healing.
2. To identify and express thoughts and feelings regarding the abuse.

## ADDITIONAL HOMEWORK THAT MAY BE APPLICABLE TO CHILD SEXUAL ABUSE

## ADDITIONAL PROBLEMS IN WHICH THIS EXERCISE MAY BE USEFUL

- Domestic Violence[*]
- Marital Affair[*]
- Physical Abuse

## SUGGESTIONS FOR PROCESSING THIS EXERCISE WITH THE CLIENT

When a child has been sexually abused, other family members need to express their own thoughts and feelings about what happened. This helps them to be available emotionally to comfort the child who has been abused. When the perpetrator is a family member who lives in the house, oftentimes the home environment is similar to having an elephant in the living room: Everyone walks around it. You need to get the family to express the thoughts, feelings, and expectations that they have of each other and especially the perpetrator. Each family member has his/her own story, which needs to be expressed and heard. The following questions can help in accomplishing this.

---

[*]These problems are not specifically discussed in detail in this volume

# GETTING IT OUT

It is a tragedy whenever a child is sexually abused. It takes a lot of time and support to overcome such an experience. As a family, in order to provide that support, each of you must be able to get a handle on your thoughts and feelings. This is also true for the person who was abused. For you to move from victim to survivor, you need to process this experience. The following exercise is a place to start for each of you to identify and express your thoughts and feelings.

## FOR THE NONABUSED FAMILY MEMBERS

1. How did I feel about _____ (person abused) before I knew s/he was abused? _____

   _____

   _____

   _____

2. How did I feel about _____ (perpetrator) before I knew he/she committed the abuse?

   _____

   _____

   _____

   _____

3. How do I feel now about _____ (person who was abused)?

   _____

   _____

   _____

   _____

4. How do I feel now about _____ (perpetrator)?

   _____

   _____

_____
_____

5.  What do I think about what happened?

_____
_____
_____
_____

6.  What questions does it raise in my mind?

_____
_____
_____

7.  How has the abuse changed my relationship with _____ (person abused)? _____

_____
_____
_____

8.  How has my relationship changed with _____ (perpetrator)?

_____
_____
_____

9.  What is the worst thing that the abuse has done to the family?

_____
_____
_____

10. How do I see my family overcoming this experience?

_____
_____

## FOR THE PERSON WHO WAS ABUSED

1.  How did I feel about the person who abused me prior to the abuse?

_____

_____

_____

_____

2.  How did I feel about myself before the abuse?

_____

_____

_____

_____

3.  How do I feel about myself now?

_____

_____

_____

_____

4.  What do I think about what happened? What questions does it raise in my mind?

_____

_____

_____

_____

_____

5.  How has the abuse changed my relationship with the perpetrator? How do I feel about this? _____

_____

_____

_____

_____

6.  How has the abuse changed my relationship with the other family members? How do I feel about this?

_____

_____

_____

_____

_____

7. What was the worst thing about the abuse?

_____

_____

_____

_____

_____

8. If there was physical contact, how do you feel about your body?

_____

_____

_____

_____

9. How do I see myself overcoming what happened to me?

_____

_____

_____

_____

10. What is the best thing about me?

_____

_____

_____

_____

# I GOTTA STOP THINKING THIS WAY

## GOALS OF THE EXERCISE

1. To identify your common thinking errors and develop more adaptive self-talk.
2. To begin a process of healing.

## ADDITIONAL HOMEWORK THAT MAY BE APPLICABLE TO CHILD SEXUAL ABUSE

- My Safe Place                                          Page 19
- Why Am I So Angry?                                     Page 26
- Go Blow Out Some Candles                               Page 36
- What Am I Thinking When I Am Feeling Depressed?        Page 115
- Creating a Positive Outlook                            Page 227

## ADDITIONAL PROBLEMS FOR WHICH THIS EXERCISE MAY BE USEFUL

- Domestic Violence[*]
- Physical Abuse[*]

## SUGGESTIONS FOR PROCESSING THIS EXERCISE WITH THE CLIENT

When a child has been abused, a range of emotions of varying levels of intensity quickly develop. These emotions usually unfold when the abuse starts. The following exercise lists some of the more common thoughts that arise. Have your client identify any emotions that apply to him/her and generate alternative, more adaptive thoughts.

---

[*]These problems are not specifically discussed in detail in this volume.

# I GOTTA STOP THINKING THIS WAY

## FOR THE PERSON WHO WAS ABUSED

This exercise is designed to help you rid yourself of negative thoughts about what happened to you. The list of faulty beliefs/thoughts is based on the thoughts/beliefs held and reported frequently by others who have also been abused like you. See if you can offer alternative and more positive thoughts/beliefs for each one listed here.

| Faulty Beliefs/Thoughts | More Realistic/Positive Thoughts |
| --- | --- |
| 1.  It was my fault. | _____ |
| 2.  I can't trust others. | _____ |
| 3.  I can't trust myself. | _____ |
| 4.  I am bad. | _____ |
| 5.  My body betrayed me. | _____ |
| 6.  I can't protect myself. | _____ |
| 7.  Sex is dirty. | _____ |
| 8.  I have to be in control. | _____ |
| 9.  I must be gay. | _____ |
| 10.  I should have never told anyone about the abuse. | _____ |

# A PICTURE IS WORTH A THOUSAND WORDS

## GOALS OF THE EXERCISE

1.  For younger children to express their thoughts and feelings.
2.  To begin a process of healing.

## ADDITIONAL HOMEWORK THAT MAY BE APPLICABLE
## TO CHILD SEXUAL ABUSE

*   My Safe Place                                         Page 19
*   Why Am I So Angry?                                    Page 26
*   Go Blow Out Some Candles                              Page 36
*   What Am I Thinking When I Am Feeling Depressed?       Page 115
*   Creating a Positive Outlook                           Page 227

## ADDITIONAL PROBLEMS FOR WHICH THIS EXERCISE MAY BE USEFUL

*   Domestic Violence*
*   Physical Abuse*

## SUGGESTIONS FOR PROCESSING THIS EXERCISE WITH THE CLIENT

When treating younger children, oftentimes it is easier for them to draw a picture of their thoughts and feelings than to express them in words. Encourage parents to spend some time with their child who has been abused and ask him/her to draw pictures of the people and places listed in the following exercises. These pictures should then be shared with the therapist.

---

*These problems are not specifically discussed in detail in this volume.

# A PICTURE IS WORTH A THOUSAND WORDS

## FOR THE ABUSED CHILD'S PARENT(S) AND THE CHILD

Arrange for some special one-on-one time with your child and ask him or her to draw pictures of people and places listed on the following pages. These pictures should then be shared with the therapist.

1.   Draw a picture of yourself.

2.   Draw a picture of a place that makes you feel safe and happy.

3.  Draw a picture of a person (or people) you trust and who makes you feel good.

4. If you can, try and draw a picture of the person who abused you.

# I AM STILL DANNY

## GOALS OF THE EXERCISE

1. Family members discontinue blaming each other or resenting the family member who is gay.
2. Feelings of conflict and rejection are resolved and a plan of acceptance is embraced.
3. Family members develop a sense of understanding and acceptance for the family member's sexuality.

## ADDITIONAL HOMEWORK THAT MAY BE APPLICABLE TO SEXUAL PREFERENCES

- When I Feel Anxious It Is Like . . .        Page 42
- How Can I Talk So He'll Listen?           Page 89
- Circles of Perception                     Page 122

## ADDITIONAL PROBLEMS FOR WHICH THIS EXERCISE MAY BE USEFUL

- Blended Families
- Divorce
- Unwanted/Unplanned Pregnancies

## SUGGESTIONS FOR PROCESSING THIS EXERCISE WITH THE CLIENT

The acceptance of alternative sexual lifestyles has been increasing over the years. Within some families, however, feelings of anger, resentment, and rejection remain strong. Such feelings arise for various reasons and could be explored within treatment sessions. Ultimately an individual needs to decide whether s/he will disclose this information to her/his family and friends (as well as which family members and which friends). Once the individual's orientation is disclosed, those made aware need to decide whether, and to what degree, they will accept that individual.

# I AM STILL DANNY

1. An individual may be having difficulty deciding whether or not to tell his/her family about his/her sexual preference, or the family may be having difficulty accepting this news. Consequently, it is helpful to identify the fears each person has regarding such information (e.g., what will our friends think?). In addition to coping with fears, it is also important for individuals to identify the many other feelings that can become ignited regarding the issue of an alternative sexual lifestyle. Suggest to family members that they generate a list of the various fears as well as other feelings and thoughts. For example,

   When I heard the news I felt _____

   It made me think _____

2. All family members need to be able to express such feelings and their accompanying thoughts to one another. This can be done by writing a letter or by communicating in person. Before doing so, it might be beneficial for individuals to think about and practice what they want to say as well as what they expect to hear. To aid the process of acceptance, each family member should answer the questions associated with his/her fears and other thoughts and feelings. For example,

   | *Questions/Fear/Feeling/Thought* | *Response* |
   |---|---|
   | What if my friends think that I am gay or don't believe that I am not? | I know that I am not gay, besides, my true/close friends wouldn't care either way. |

3. Sometimes individuals cannot approve of or agree with a family member's sexual choice. In order for a relationship to survive, there needs to be a sense of acceptance. Each of you needs to keep in mind your feelings for the member who is choosing an alternative sexual lifestyle. Describe/list the reasons you loved him/her before he/she expressed his/her sexual preference.

4. For the next week, focus only on the qualities beyond the sexuality of the family member. Focus on those qualities and how they may weigh against the issue of sexual preference.

# I WANT THINGS TO BE BETTER

## GOALS OF THE EXERCISE

1. To reduce and eliminate thoughts and feelings about suicide or hurting oneself.
2. To instill a sense of hope in the person thinking about suicide.
3. To help the individual feeling/thinking this way to develop a better understanding as to how such thoughts and feelings develop.
4. To generate alternative plans to suicide or hurting oneself.

## ADDITIONAL HOMEWORK THAT MAY BE APPLICABLE TO SUICIDE ATTEMPTS

- My Safe Place                                                   Page 19
- A Picture Is Worth a Thousand Words (just pictures 1–3)         Page 215
- What Am I Thinking When I Am Feeling Depressed?                 Page 115
- What Do Others Value about Me?                                  Page 117
- Creating a Positive Outlook                                     Page 227

## ADDITIONAL PROBLEMS IN WHICH THIS EXERCISE MAY BE USEFUL

- Addictions
- Anxiety
- Depression
- Family Conflict[*]

## SUGGESTIONS FOR PROCESSING THIS EXERCISE WITH THE CLIENT

Many individuals thinking about suicide or wanting to hurt themselves feel that there is no hope of things changing. It is important to convey to these people that there are options and that things can get better. To do this, it is also important for such individuals to become more aware of the triggers to such thoughts and feelings. The following exercise is designed to do this and to generate a prevention plan.

---

[*]This problem is not specifically discussed in detail in this volume.

# I WANT THINGS TO BE BETTER

I am glad that you are taking the time to read this. That demonstrates that a part of you does want things to be better. Once you complete this exercise, you will have a plan of how you can take charge of making things better for you.

1.  When you feel or think about suicide/hurting yourself, what has usually happened before you started thinking or feeling this way?

    _____

    _____

    _____

    _____

    _____

    _____

2.  Describe the thoughts and feelings you experience during such times.

    _____

    _____

    _____

    _____

    _____

3.  Where were you when you started to think/feel this way?

    _____

    _____

    _____

    _____

    _____

4.  What did you do?

    _____
    _____
    _____
    _____
    _____
    _____

5.  How did you feel after you did this?

    _____
    _____
    _____
    _____

6.  In what way was your behavior, as well as the thoughts and feelings you had,
    helpful? _____

    _____
    _____
    _____
    _____

7.  What is the negative side to such behavior, thoughts, and feelings?

    _____
    _____
    _____
    _____
    _____

8.  When else have you felt or thought this way but did not try to hurt yourself?

    _____
    _____
    _____
    _____

9.  What thoughts and/or behaviors stopped you from hurting yourself?

    _____

    _____

    _____

    _____

    _____

    _____

10. What other things (people, activities, thoughts) have helped you to reduce the thoughts and/or feelings of wanting to hurt yourself?

    _____

    _____

    _____

    _____

    _____

    _____

11. What else would help you to reduce such thoughts/feelings?

    _____

    _____

    _____

    _____

    _____

    _____

12. Make a list of all the things that would help you reduce and possibly eliminate such thoughts and feelings (e.g., reminding yourself that this feeling will not last forever, spending time with a supportive friend or family member).

    _____

    _____

    _____

    _____

    _____

    _____

13. Describe how you would feel and what thoughts you would have while doing the things you just listed in item 12.

   _____

   _____

   _____

   _____

   _____

   _____

# CREATING A POSITIVE OUTLOOK

## GOALS OF THE EXERCISE

1. To generate a sense of hope.
2. To identify the positives in one's life (or reasons for living).
3. To recognize who the support people are in your life.

## ADDITIONAL HOMEWORK THAT MAY BE APPLICABLE TO SUICIDE ATTEMPTS

## ADDITIONAL PROBLEMS FOR WHICH THIS EXERCISE MAY BE USEFUL

- Depression
- Family Conflict*

## SUGGESTIONS FOR PROCESSING THIS EXERCISE WITH THE CLIENT

Individuals experiencing thoughts and feelings about suicide or a wish to harm oneself need to develop a sense of optimism and positiveness in their lives. They need to focus in on the things in their lives that are and have been good. These can involve memories of good times they've shared with others, times they accomplished something positive or worthwhile, or times when they received something they really wanted. Encouraging individuals to focus on identifying such thoughts and feelings gives credence to the belief that life can be good and has not been ALL bad.

---

*This problem is not specifically discussed in detail in this volume.

# CREATING A POSITIVE OUTLOOK

You are now on your way to making things better for yourself. After completing this exercise, you will have created a more positive outlook for yourself and your future.

1.  Describe a time you laughed really hard.

    _____

    _____

    _____

    _____

    _____

    _____

2.  Describe a time you completed something well (e.g., got a high mark on a test, scored a point in a game, received a compliment).

    _____

    _____

    _____

    _____

    _____

    _____

3.  Identify and describe two or three people who make you feel good.

    _____

    _____

    _____

    _____

    _____

    _____

4. Identify and describe at least three things that you do that make you feel good.

_____

_____

_____

_____

_____

_____

5. In the next week, schedule a time when you will do at least two of the things that you listed in item 4. _____

**Time**

Sunday _____

Monday _____

Tuesday _____

Wednesday _____

Thursday _____

Friday _____

Saturday _____

6. Describe a plan of how you will spend more time with the people you identified in item 3 and how you can do what you identified in item 5 more often.

_____

_____

_____

_____

_____

_____

# HONEY, GUESS WHAT?

## GOALS OF THE EXERCISE

1. Unite/reunite family relationships by being able to express individual thoughts and feelings about the unplanned pregnancy.
2. Identify and demonstrate ways of being supportive to one another (especially the individual who is pregnant).
3. Formulate a plan of what to do (e.g., having the child and deciding how to raise him/her, pursuing adoption, or other alternatives).

## ADDITIONAL HOMEWORK THAT MAY BE APPLICABLE TO UNWANTED/UNPLANNED PREGNANCIES

- Should We or Should We Not?       Page 153

## ADDITIONAL PROBLEMS FOR WHICH THIS EXERCISE MAY BE USEFUL

- Multiple-Birth Dilemmas

## SUGGESTIONS FOR PROCESSING THIS EXERCISE WITH CLIENT

An unplanned pregnancy can be both a joyous surprise and a scary and gut-wrenching dilemma. When an unexpected pregnancy emerges within couple or family treatment, the decision of what to do can be overwhelmingly difficult to determine. Regardless of the decision, support and communication regarding the various feelings and thoughts that arise are essential. The following homework is a guideline for how to process such a dilemma.

# HONEY, GUESS WHAT?

Support and communication regarding the various thoughts and feelings that one has about pregnancy are always essential. The following homework exercise is a guideline for how you can maintain/create the support you need at this particular time. In completing it, you will also open up the lines of communication, in order to express the various thoughts and feelings and needs that each of you have regarding your pregnancy.

1. Each family member is to identify the various thoughts and feelings he/she has regarding the pregnancy. Record these on paper.

2. Remember to use "I" statements and to refrain from any blaming or derogatory remarks.

3. Schedule a family meeting, and have each member share his/her thoughts and feelings. If this creates chaos, have a family session so that your therapist can facilitate the process.

Once you have completed the above, proceed to the next step.

4. Throughout the next week, each family member is to imagine having a baby in the home. Family members can talk to others (family, friends, or a support group) regarding how things will be different once a baby arrives, and how each person and the family as a whole will be affected.

Once you have completed this, try the next step.

5. Brainstorm a list of the pros and cons for all options considered.

| Option | Pros | Cons |
| --- | --- | --- |
| _____ | _____ | _____ |
| _____ | _____ | _____ |
| _____ | _____ | _____ |
| _____ | _____ | _____ |
| _____ | _____ | _____ |

6.  Decide on an option and describe who will do what.

    _____

    _____

    _____

    _____

    _____

7.  Identify individuals who are considered supportive to the person who is pregnant and to other family members who are affected and involved. My support people are:

    _____

    _____

    _____

8.  Have each member describe ways he/she wants support, reassurance, comfort, and so forth regarding the decision made.

    _____

    _____

    _____

    _____

    _____

    _____

# REFERENCES

Alberti, R., & Emmons, M. (2001). *Your perfect right.* Atascadero, CA: Impact.

Christensen, A., & Jacobson, N. S. (2000). *Reconcilable differences.* New York: Guilford Press.

Dattilio, F. M. (2007). Breaking the pattern of interruption in family therapy. *The Family Journal 15*(2), 163–165.

Dattilio, F. M. (2010). *Cognitive-behavior therapy with couples and families: A comprehensive guide for clinicians.* New York: Guilford.

Dattilio, F. M., & Dickson, J. (2007). Assigning homework to couples and families. *Cognitive and Behavioral Practice, 14*(3), 268–277.

Dattilio, F. M., & Nichols, M. P. (2010). Reuniting estranged family members: A cognitive-behavioral-systemic perspective. *American Journal of Family Therapy* (in press).

Dattilio, F. M., Kazantzis, N., Shinkfield, G., & Carr, A. (2010). Survey of homework use and barriers impeding homework completion in couples and family therapy. *Journal of Marital and Family Therapy* (in press).

Epstein, N. B., & Baucom, D. H. (2007). Couples. In N. Kazantzis & L. L'Abate (Eds.), *Handbook of homework assignments in psychotherapy: Research, practice, prevention* (pp. 187–201). New York: Springer.

Kellogg, S. H., & Young, J. E. (2008). *Cognitive therapy.* In J. L. Lebow's, *Twenty-first century psychotherapies: Contemporary approaches to theory and practice* (pp. 43–79). Hoboken, NJ: John Wiley & Sons.

L'Abate, L., & Cusinato, M. (2007). Linking theory with practice: Theory-driven interventions in prevention and family therapy. *The Family Journal, 15*(4), 318–327.

Linville, D., & Hertlein, K. M. (Eds.). (2007). *The therapist's notebook for family health care: Homework, handouts, and activities for individuals, couples, and families coping with illness, loss, and disability.* New York: Haworth Press.

Zinbarg, R. E., & Griffith, N. (2008). Behavior therapy. In J. L. Lebow's, *Twenty-first century psychotherapies: Contemporary approaches to theory and practice* (pp. 8–42). Hoboken, NJ: John Wiley & Sons.

# ABOUT THE AUTHORS

**Louis J. Bevilacqua, Psy.D.**, is a Clinical Psychologist and Vice President of Life Counseling Services (LCS), which has over 25 office locations throughout Pennsylvania, New Jersey, and Florida. Dr. Bevilacqua is the Internship Training Director at LCS, which is an APPIC approved training program. He is the Executive Director of The Light Program, a Mental Health Intensive Outpatient Program which serves adolescents and adults, as well as individuals suffering from eating-disorder behaviors. The Light Program is offered throughout Pennsylvania and New Jersey. Dr. Bevilacqua received his doctorate in Clinical Psychology at The Philadelphia College of Osteopathic Medicine under the direction of Arthur Freeman, Ed.D., ABPP. Dr. Bevilacqua specializes in Cognitive-Behavioral Therapy of mood disorders, family therapy, and treating self-injurious behaviors. His other publications include *Comparative Treatments for Relationship Dysfunction* and the first edition of *The Brief Family Therapy Homework Planner,* both co-edited with Frank Dattilio, Ph.D., ABPP, as well as *The Group Therapy Homework Planner.*

**Frank M. Dattilio, Ph.D., ABPP**, is one of the leading figures in Cognitive-Behavior Therapy (CBT) in the world. He holds a joint faculty position with the Department of Psychiatry at Harvard Medical School and the University of Pennsylvania School of Medicine. He is also in private practice of clinical psychology and marital and family therapy in Allentown, Pennsylvania. Dr. Dattilio is a licensed psychologist who is listed in the National Register of Health Service Providers in Psychology. He is board certified in both clinical psychology and behavioral psychology with the American Board of Professional Psychology and is a clinical member of the American Association for Marriage and Family Therapists. He has also served as a visiting faculty member at several major universities throughout the world.

Dr. Dattilio trained in behavior therapy through the department of psychiatry at Temple University School of Medicine under the direction of the late Joseph Wolpe, M.D., and was awarded a postdoctoral fellowship through the Center for Cognitive Therapy at the University of Pennsylvania School of Medicine, under the direction of Aaron T. Beck, M.D.

Dr. Dattilio has more than 250 professional publications in the areas of anxiety and behavioral disorders, forensic and clinical psychology, and marital and family discord. He has presented extensively throughout the United States, Canada, Africa, Asia, Europe, South America, Australia, New Zealand, Mexico, the West Indies, and Cuba on cognitive-behavior therapy. His works have been translated into more than 28 languages and are used in over 80 countries.

# ABOUT THE CD-ROM

## INTRODUCTION

This appendix provides you with the information on the contents of the CD that accompanies this book. For the latest and greatest information, please refer to the ReadMe file located at the root of the CD.

## SYSTEM REQUIREMENTS

- A computer with a processor running at 120 Mhz or faster
- At least 32 MB of total RAM installed on your computer; for best performance, we recommend at least 64MB
- A CD-ROM drive

*Note:* Many popular word processing programs are capable of reading Microsoft Word files. However, users should be aware that a slight amount of formatting might be lost when using a program other than Microsoft Word.

## USING THE CD WITH WINDOWS

To install the items from the CD to your hard drive, follow these steps:

1. Insert the CD into your computer's CD-ROM drive.
2. The CD-ROM interface will appear. The interface provides a simple point-and-click way to explore the contents of the CD.

If the opening screen of the CD-ROM does not appear automatically, follow these steps to access the CD:

1. Click the Start button on the left end of the taskbar and then choose Run from the menu that pops up. (In Windows Vista and Windows 7, skip this step.)
2. In the dialog box that appears, **type d:\setup.exe**. (If your CD-ROM drive is not drive d, fill in the appropriate letter in place of d.) This brings up the CD interface described in the preceding set of steps. (In Windows Vista or Windows 7, type d:\setup.exe in the Start > Search text box.)

## USING THE CD WITH A MAC

1. Insert the CD into your computer's CD-ROM drive.
2. The CD-ROM icon appears on your desktop, double-click the icon.
3. Double-click the Start icon.
4. The CD-ROM interface will appear. The interface provides a simple point-and-click way to explore the contents of the CD.

## WHAT'S ON THE CD

The following sections provide a summary of the software and other materials you'll find on the CD.

### Content

Includes all 78 homework assignments from the book in Word format. Homework assignments can be customized, printed out, and distributed to clients in an effort to extend the therapeutic process outside the office. All documentation is included in the folder named "Content."

### Applications

The following application is on the CD:

### OpenOffice.org

OpenOffice.org is a free multi-platform office productivity suite. It is similar to Microsoft Office or Lotus SmartSuite, but OpenOffice.org is absolutely free. It includes word processing, spreadsheet, presentation, and drawing applications that enable you to create professional documents, newsletters, reports, and presentations. It supports most file formats of other office software. You should be able to edit and view any files created with other office solutions. Certain features of Microsoft Word documents may not display as expected from within OpenOffice.org. For system requirements, go to www.openoffice.org.

### Software can be of the following types:

- Shareware programs are fully functional, free, trial versions of copyrighted programs. If you like particular programs, register with their authors for a nominal fee and receive licenses, enhanced versions, and technical support.
- Freeware programs are free, copyrighted games, applications, and utilities. You can copy them to as many computers as you like—for free—but they offer no technical support.
- GNU software is governed by its own license, which is included inside the folder of the GNU software. There are no restrictions on distribution of GNU software. See the GNU license at the root of the CD for more details.

- Trial, demo, or evaluation versions of software are usually limited either by time or functionality (such as not letting you save a project after you create it).

## Troubleshooting

If you have difficulty installing or using any of the materials on the companion CD, try the following solutions:

- **Turn off any antivirus software that you may have running.** Installers sometimes mimic virus activity and can make your computer incorrectly believe that a virus is infecting it. (Be sure to turn the antivirus software back on later.)
- **Close all running programs.** The more programs that you're running, the less memory is available to other programs. Installers also typically update files and programs; if you keep other programs running, installation may not work properly.
- **Reference the README file.** Please refer to the README file located at the root of the CD for the latest product information at the time of publication.

## USER ASSISTANCE

If you have trouble with the CD-ROM, please call the Wiley Product Technical Support phone number at (800) 762-2974. Outside the United States, call 1 (317) 572-3994. You can also contact Wiley Product Technical Support at http://support.wiley.com. John Wiley & Sons will provide technical support only for installation and other general quality control items. For technical support of the applications themselves, consult the program vendor or author.

To place additional orders or to request information about other Wiley products, please call (800) 225-5945.